# BBC
# DOCTOR WHO
# THE VISUAL DICTIONARY

Gray hair lends older appearance

Fitted coat with red silk lining

Simple outfit chosen by newly regenerated Doctor

Two hearts

New kidneys are not a color that the Doctor likes

Signet ring

Meticulously polished shoes

THE TWELFTH DOCTOR

**SONTARAN DEVICE**

Activation button

Blue lights signify activation

**SONIC SCREWDRIVER**

Casing frazzled from using too much power to attract the Atraxi

**WARP STAR**

Carbonized shell

Crystal contains enough power to explode a space station

**THE DOCTOR'S GALLIFREYAN CRADLE**

Solar-system themed mobile

Gallifreyan writing possibly spells the Doctor's name

Ancient wooden crib worn with age

Clear fluid reduces risk of dehydration

Saturnyne blood transforms cellular structure from human to Saturnyne

Blood for transfusion flows through fine tubes

Cuff restrains victim during transfusion

Shackle binds victim's ankle

**SATURNYNE CHAIR**

**DNA SCANNER**

Rotating nodes go "ding"

Electronic odds and ends hold device together

**OOD OPERATIONS PRESS PACK**

Map of the company's complex

a simple guide of written communication with your ood

**operations**

ood

new price cut
only 50 credits
BUY ONE NOW

Vouchers for the office canteen

**FREEDOM FIGHTER GUN**

Enhanced targeting gear

Stun ray muzzle

Device is used to send and receive voice messages

WRIST
COMMUNICATION
UNIT

# BBC
# DOCTOR WHO
## THE VISUAL DICTIONARY

Written by JASON LOBORIK, NEIL CORRY, JACQUELINE RAYNER,
ANDREW DARLING, KERRIE DOUGHERTY, DAVID JOHN, and SIMON BEECROFT

Antigravity device allows robot to hover in midair

Coils capable of incinerating victims

ROBOTIC
ANTIBODY

Visor reflects landscape of Utah desert

American flag

Interior of suit contains alien intelligence technology and built-in communication faculties

Stolen 1960s Apollo astronaut suit

Casings trap River inside suit

Shape of the Ood Operations company logo

OOD OPERATIONS
SCULPTURE

RIVER SONG'S
SPACESUIT

Living figure grown from Androzani trees

WOODEN QUEEN

ABZORBALOFF
CANE

DK

# CONTENTS

# MYSTERIOUS VISITOR

TIME AND TIME AGAIN, fate seems to thrust a mysterious time traveler, known as the Doctor, into the right place at the right time. However, because the Doctor always arrives at times of catastrophe, some legends have evolved to suggest that he is the cause of these events. In fact, he is usually instrumental in the resolution of crises, but like a storm, he can also leave damage in his wake. The Doctor was a crucial figure in the Last Great Time War between the Daleks and the Time Lords in which, for the sake of the universe, he was driven to bring about the destruction of the Daleks in order to save the Time Lords and his home planet, Gallifrey. The Doctor continues to appear where he is needed to alleviate the chaos created in both time and space.

THE DOCTOR

## Target: Earth

Many alien races have sought to invade Earth, to enslave humanity, rob it of its mineral wealth, or simply destroy the planet. Displaced beings, such as the Nestene Consciousness, Gelth, and the Zygons, have sought refuge on Earth, while the Daleks have made it the focus of many attacks, once even towing it to another galaxy. A megalomaniac Time Lord, known as the Master, has twice tried to conquer Earth and make it a launch pad to wage war on the universe. Fortunately for humanity, the Doctor has often defeated these plans and saved the world.

England, and London in particular, have seen more than a few attempts at alien invasion. However, few citizens of the 20th or 21st centuries would be aware of them, thanks to the efforts of UNIT and the Torchwood Institute. These are Earth-based organizations that defeat and cover up alien threats.

## The Super Highway

The Doctor travels in a TARDIS—an advanced piece of Time Lord technology that can time travel. His Type 40 ship looks like a 1950s police box. TARDISes move from one moment or place to another by passing through the time vortex: a swirling mass of energy that links all points in time and space.

Earth eventually dies in the year 5.5/Apple/26. It is destroyed naturally by the expanding Sun, not by an enemy.

As humankind spreads out into galaxies farther afield, they have cause to be grateful for the presence of the Doctor there too. On the planet Trenzalore, which the Doctor defended for centuries, the children drew pictures of the Doctor's greatest adventures as a gift to thank him for saving them.

# RENEGADE TIME LORD

**T**HE DOCTOR believes himself to be the last surviving Time Lord—a long-lived and incredibly technologically advanced race that possesses the secret of time travel. The Time Lords preferred to observe the universe and rarely interfered in the affairs of other worlds, whereas the Doctor has a strong sense of right and wrong, and a firm conviction that he should intervene to prevent injustice. Unable to agree with a policy of non-intervention, the Doctor became a renegade, stealing a TARDIS and using it to explore time and space.

## There is Only One Doctor

When Time Lords come to the end of their lives, they have the ability to regenerate their bodies and carry on living. Although each regeneration brings out different facets of a Time Lord's personality, the Doctor's essential character has remained unchanged for centuries.

The Doctor's playful, occasionally child-like traits conceal an extensive knowledge of the universe and deep wisdom born of experience. In his newest regenerative form, he prefers to listen and think before acting—to learn the measure of the many aliens he encounters around the universe.

## Mythical Hero

The Doctor's appearances on Earth and services to humanity have gone down in legend and references to him are scattered throughout folklore. The "Man in the Blue Box" takes on an almost religious significance in this stained glass window from a London church.

The TARDIS

The Doctor has a gift for appearing at critical moments in time when catastrophe is about to strike, including the launch of the *Titanic* and at the eruption of Krakatoa in Indonesia.

POLICE PUBLIC CALL BOX

POLICE TELEPHONE
FREE
FOR USE OF
PUBLIC
ADVICE & ASSISTANCE
OBTAINABLE IMMEDIATELY
OFFICERS & CARS
RESPOND TO ALL CALLS
PULL TO OPEN

## Traveling Through Time

The gift of time travel also brings responsibility. The rules of time are fluid and complicated. Actions have consequences, and not all time is in flux—some tragedies cannot be reversed.

### Maintaining Time

The Doctor has prevented catastrophe from rewriting the future of Earth many times. He sees his relationship with humans as a strength, but his enemies regard it as a weakness that is easy to exploit. By threatening Earth during World War II, the Daleks know that Winston Churchill will call his good friend the Doctor, who walks straight into the trap.

### Missed Opportunities

Some moments are temporal tipping points, where decisive action could create a new timeline. When the future pivots around human-Silurian negotiations for a cohabitation deal, the Doctor is hopeful for a new era on Earth. Sadly, talks break down, the Silurians return to hibernation and life on Earth continues as before.

### Fixed Points

Some events are fixed and cannot be changed. The Doctor can only mourn and carry on. On Bowie Base One, the Doctor refuses to follow the rules of time and rescues the crew. But base leader, Adelaide Brooke, was destined to die. She insists on maintaining the fixed order of things and so kills herself.

### Man's Best Friend

The Doctor feels a special affinity for the human race. Even though he has witnessed the very worst of human behavior, he is still awed by their potential for goodness. He cannot bear to stand by and watch humanity suffer—especially if children are crying.

The Doctor believes that the moment you pick up a weapon, you have lost the argument. He always looks for a peaceful solution first, trying to negotiate or give aliens a choice. For example, when confronted with the Saturnynes' plan to sink Venice, he tries to reason with Rosanna Calvierri. However, he often finds himself in situations where violent action is necessary. He destroys the Saturnynes because they won't abandon their plan and they show such little respect for the human beings in their care.

Despite his vibrant personality, the Doctor is sometimes overwhelmed by his belief that he is the last surviving Time Lord. He has developed strong relationships with many humans, but they are limited because of his extraordinary longevity and the fact that his life is fraught with danger. He leads a solitary life, punctuated by the company of people who travel with him, but who must always return to their own lives.

## THE DOCTOR FACTS

- The Doctor's body temperature is a cool 59-61 degrees Fahrenheit (15–16 Celsius), lower than the typical human body temperature of 98.6 degrees Fahrenheit (37 Celsius).

- This Time Lord is qualified in "practically everything," but has never actually received a medical degree.

- He was a member of a Time Lord clan called the Prydonian Chapter. This was said to be the most powerful and devious of all the chapters.

- At the Prydonian Academy, the young Doctor just scraped through with a 51 percent pass, and it was on his second attempt.

- River Song may be the only non-Gallifreyan to know the Doctor's real name, although the Doctor claims that it is unpronounceable for humans. His nickname at the Prydonian Academy was "Theta Sigma."

# ANATOMY OF THE DOCTOR

ALTHOUGH HE LOOKS LIKE a human being (and once claimed human ancestry on his mother's side), the Doctor is an alien being and his Time Lord physiology has many differences from our own. Physically, the Doctor is stronger, has sharper senses, and greater powers of endurance than a human being, and can cope with heat, cold, radiation and powerful forces better than humans can. There are also some differences to his internal anatomy that have confused many Earthly doctors.

## Two Hearts

Time Lords have two hearts and a binary vascular system, which enables them to survive major accidents and many physical and temporal shocks that would kill a human being. They also have a respiratory bypass system that enables them to survive without breathing for some time.

Time Lord life-energy is tremendously vibrant and powerful. When the TARDIS's power supply is almost totally destroyed, save for one cell, the Tenth Doctor recharges it by breathing his own life energy into the remaining power cell, giving up 10 years of his life in the process.

Nutrient fluid preserves severed hand

## The Doctor's Hand

When the Doctor's right hand is severed by a Sycorax warrior, residual regeneration energy allows him to grow another. His friend Captain Jack acquires the original, and the liquid surrounding it bubbles whenever the Doctor or a product of his DNA is near. Later, after a run-in with a Dalek triggers the Doctor's regeneration process, he blasts his regeneration energy into his severed hand, healing himself without having to change appearance—but effectively using up one whole regeneration.

Body can absorb Roentgen radiation, endure massive gamma radiation strikes, and survive cyanide poisoning

The Doctor's clothes help him appear non-threatening to humans

Body temperature is lower than a human's

Two hearts are supported by a binary vascular system

Enhanced sense of taste can identify different blood groups

Heightened senses can pinpoint historical eras by smell

Eye color can change with regeneration

Thick eyebrows appear, according to the Doctor, to look angry of their own accord

Gray hair, not red as the Doctor might prefer

Highly developed Time Lord brain has huge memory capacity and telepathic ability

New face chosen by the Doctor, although he cannot initially remember why

Respiratory bypass system allows short-term survival in airless environments

## Two Doctors

A new version of the Doctor is created after a biological metacrisis combines genetic information from the Doctor's severed hand and from the human Donna Noble, with energy from an abortive regeneration. Although he looks like the Tenth Doctor, this half-Time Lord and half-human creation has only one heart and is unable to regenerate.

The Doctor's capacity to regenerate is limited. It can be increased or halted – as shown when his Time Lord nemesis, the Master, temporarily suspends the Doctor's ability to change. Without his regenerative abilities, the Doctor's body would be more than 900 years old, so he becomes a tiny wizened creature as he reaches his true age.

Clothes shrunk to fit miniature Tenth Doctor

### WIZENED TENTH DOCTOR

As a Time Lord, the Doctor relies on different bacteria from humans to keep him alive. Not knowing this, the Silurians begin a decontamination process on him to neutralize what they diagnose as harmful germs and viruses in his system—leaving him screaming in agony.

### THE DREAM LORD

Physically, the Doctor is stronger than any human, but psychologically, he is just as vulnerable. Owing to his long and dramatic life, he's seen many dark things. When psychic pollen gets into the TARDIS machinery, it induces a dream state for the Doctor, Amy, and Rory. It feeds on the Doctor's fears and insecurities. This malign manifestation calls itself the Dream Lord, and revels in taunting the Doctor and playing games of life and death.

The Dream Lord wears a smarter version of the Eleventh Doctor's clothes

## A Minimalist Approach

Every time the Doctor regenerates, he selects an outfit to suit his new personality. Now more than 2,000 years old, the Twelfth Doctor sought a more sedate look than his previous incarnations. He was aiming for minimalist, but worries he looks more like a magician instead. This is a newer, fresher Doctor, who has turned away from the younger, more quirky styles of his previous incarnations.

Comfortable, thick-soled shoes suitable for running—useful when making a quick escape

# REGENERATION

IN CASES OF ADVANCED age, mortal illness, or fatal injury, Time Lords have the ability to regenerate their bodies to create a new physical form. There is a notable shift in personality too, due to chemical changes in the brain. The regeneration process takes many hours. It is hugely traumatic and can cause mental and psychological instability until it is completed.

As cellular restructure begins, the Doctor's body starts to glow with regeneration energy. The process might begin with the hands morphing first, for example, followed by the rest of the body.

The process of regeneration is much like dying, even though it is the same Time Lord who comes back. It is a terrifying experience because the outcome is unknown.

## REGENERATION FACTS

- Most regenerations are triggered when a Time Lord is too badly injured to survive. But some Time Lords can control the process.

- Time Lords supposedly have limited regeneration cycles—they can only regenerate 12 times, allowing for 13 bodies. However, the High Council can bend the rules.

- The regenerative process can be very painful and disorienting.

- The Doctor's arch enemy, the Master has regenerated numerous times in order to cheat death.

- It might be possible for a Time Lord to choose the form he or she regenerates into.

Youthful demeanor

Unlike previous regenerations inside the TARDIS, when the Tenth Doctor regenerates it creates havoc in the spacecraft. Possibly because of the incredible amount of radiation he's absorbed, the Doctor's regeneration energy shoots out from his body with such force that it causes the console to explode. The appearance of the TARDIS's interior can also change as the Doctor gets a new physical form.

### THE TENTH DOCTOR

The Tenth Doctor finally meets his end, not at the hand of a great enemy, but when he chooses to save his companion Donna's grandfather, Wilfred Mott, from a radiation chamber. Selflessly stepping into his place, he absorbs a fatal dose of radiation—which begins the regeneration process. Although he accepts the inevitability of regeneration, the Tenth Doctor does not yet feel ready to go. This time there is no cheating the process, unlike a previous time—when he stopped his regeneration before he changed, stating that he liked his current self too much.

## Comforting Words

The telepathic Ood can see that the Tenth Doctor's death is coming. In gratitude for his rescuing them in the past, they sing to the Doctor to soothe his transition and give him strength for the agonizing process.

It is faithful companion Clara who appeals to the Time Lords to save the dying, aged Eleventh Doctor. They give him another lifecycle and he uses the excess regeneration energy to destroy the Daleks invading Trenzalore.

Having moments before believed he was facing certain death, and being willing to die for the people of Trenzalore, the Doctor welcomes this unexpected gift from the remaining Time Lords.

It's not just Time Lords that can regenerate. In certain obscure circumstances, such as exposure to energies from the TARDIS, others can absorb Time Lord abilities. The Doctor is delighted to discover that River Song, conceived in the TARDIS, can regenerate just like a Time Lord.

THE TWELFTH DOCTOR

## Growing Old

Despite their regenerative powers, Time Lords cannot fight old age forever. After spending hundreds of years defending the planet Trenzalore from alien armies, the Eleventh Doctor becomes wrinkled and gray. He knows that he has used up all his available regenerations and that, this time, death will be final—or so he thinks.

The Eleventh Doctor retains his love of human fashions, particularly bow ties, to the end

## A New Face

A new body requires a period of readjustment. Confusion, erratic behaviour and memory loss are common. The Doctor has been known to demand apples, or fish fingers dipped in custard soon after regenerating. The Twelfth Doctor just needs a suitable outfit to wear in cold Victorian London, where he finds himself after crash-landing the TARDIS.

## A Good Man?

Although there's a new face in the TARDIS, the latest version of the Doctor is still the bravest man in the universe. He uses brain over brawn, proudly defends Earth, lives life with a passion, and never hides his anger when he sees the suffering of others. The Twelfth Doctor is still the man monsters have nightmares about. Perhaps more tinged by war and sadness than before, this new incarnation is particularly concerned with whether his reputation is as a good man or a bad one.

THE ELEVENTH DOCTOR ON TRENZALORE

Raggedy clothes borrowed from man found on streets

# MANY FACES: ONE TIME LORD

TIME LORDS ORDINARILY HAVE 13 lives before their bodies are unable to regenerate any more. In this time a Time Lord can adopt many faces, be forced to change, or choose to do so. In response to extraordinary circumstances, extra lives can be bestowed.

## The Eighth Doctor

With the Time War raging between his people and the Daleks, the Eighth Doctor refuses to join the fight—until the fateful day he crash-lands on Karn. The immortal Sisterhood of Karn pleads with him to help save the universe. The Doctor eventually realizes that he has to play his part, deciding to cast off the mantle of "Doctor" and become a warrior, or the War Doctor, instead.

Ceremonial robes favored by the Sisterhood

Disheveled clothes from life spent running

## The Other Doctor

After ordinary human Jackson Lake's wife is killed by the Cybermen, he wants to forget. He finds an infostamp—a steel object for storing compressed data—but it backfires and streams facts about the Doctor into his head, causing him to believe that he is the Doctor. He may not be a Time Lord, but Lake's courage and ingenuity are genuine and gain him a companion. Brave and resourceful servant Rosita Farisi throws in her lot with him when he saves her life.

Rosita becomes nursemaid to Jackson Lake's motherless son.

Victorian gentleman's outfit

Not only does Jackson Lake believe he is the Doctor, he also calls his screwdriver a "sonic" screwdriver and builds a TARDIS—a hot air balloon he names a "Tethered Aerial Release Developed In Style".

JACKSON LAKE

ROSITA FARISI

PRIESTESS OHILA

The prophetic Sisterhood of Karn once saved the Fourth Doctor's life, and many years later, they bring his eighth incarnation back from the dead. Their leader, Ohila, believes the Doctor is the only one who can save the universe.

Priestess Ohila prepares several versions of the Elixir of Life for the Doctor. Each potion would trigger a regeneration into a different body and personality. This process makes the transformation much more painful than on previous occasions.

The First Doctor becomes worn out and changes after defeating a fierce Cyberman invasion.

The Time Lords transform the Second Doctor's appearance and exile him to Earth.

The Third Doctor dies from radiation poisoning while fighting the arachnid Great One.

The Fourth Doctor gives his life and falls to his death in order to stop the evil Master.

The Fifth Doctor's worries that he won't regenerate after being poisoned are not founded.

The Sixth Doctor regenerates after being badly injured when the TARDIS is attacked.

Jacket dirtied by battle in the Time War

Three versions of the Doctor encountering himself in the same timeline in order to stop the Time War causes a paradox anomoly. The TARDIS tries to compensate for this by refreshing its desktop and changing its interior.

Having stolen the galaxy-obliterating weapon the Moment, the War Doctor agonizes over his decision to use it—an act which would destroy billions of lives but would end the war.

## The War Doctor

Having chosen to fight as a warrior in the Time War, this tougher, battle-weary incarnation believes he has lost the right to call himself "the Doctor". He decides the only way to end the fighting is to destroy both Daleks and Time Lords, but in events that rewrite time, he instead teams up with his other selves to save his people, to their great gratification.

During the Last Day of the Time War, the War Doctor flies the TARDIS through a solid wall, crushing the Dalek army that has come searching for him.

Face and mannerisms bear striking resemblance to the Fourth Doctor

## The Twelfth Doctor

A contrast to his boyish predecessor, the older-looking Twelfth Doctor is a fearsome character with a burning passion for knowledge and adventure. It takes his friends some time to get used to him, but it's not long before his youthful energy and personality shine through.

Practical, protective leather gaiters

### THE CURATOR

An enigmatic old man, the Curator is possibly a future Doctor who has decided to revisit the form of a previous incarnation.

The Seventh Doctor is killed accidentally when a surgical probe punctures his second heart.

The dying Eighth Doctor takes the life-giving Elixir of Life to become the War Doctor.

The War Doctor realizes that his old body is wearing thin and that he must change once again.

Saving Rose from vortex energy causes the Ninth Doctor's regeneration.

Rescuing Wilfred Mott causes the Tenth Doctor to be fatally poisoned by radiation.

Having spent centuries on the planet Trenzalore, the Eleventh Doctor regenerates after reaching old age.

## Inner Beauty

The TARDIS's unremarkable external appearance conceals a vast and impressive interior. A maze of corridors lead to bedrooms, bathrooms, wardrobe rooms, attics, and much more, but the nerve center is the control room and this is where the Doctor spends most of his time. Powerful shields prevent anything from gaining access to the TARDIS, while also protecting those inside if the doors are opened during flight.

# INSIDE THE TARDIS

TIME LORD TIME-SPACE engineering allows the TARDIS to be significantly larger on the inside than on the outside. Because the TARDIS is dimensionally transcendental, its interior and exterior exist in different dimensions, and are connected by a space-time bridge at the TARDIS's entrance. The interior can be configured in almost any way as per the TARDIS pilot's wishes.

## The Eye of Harmony

The TARDIS's space-time travel is fueled by a temporal energy called Artron energy, generated both by the Eye of Harmony (an artificial black hole on Gallifrey) and by Time Lords' minds. Artron energy from the Eye was transferred to a miniature copy of the Eye and stored in the TARDIS console. In one sequence of events, to prevent the TARDIS from exploding, the Eleventh Doctor travels to the heart of the TARDIS, where the Eye of Harmony resembles a volatile star.

On the sentient planet House, the Doctor is able to build a new TARDIS out of spare parts from old, wrecked TARDISes. Consisting of a rudimentary console and powered by the female embodiment of the TARDIS matrix—Idris—the makeshift junk TARDIS was unstable, but successful, in flight.

## Famous Visitors

The usual response from astonished visitors to the TARDIS is, "It's bigger on the inside than the outside." But artist Vincent van Gogh sees things differently from most people. His first comment is about the color scheme—he likes it.

Inside the maze-like TARDIS are many customized rooms including a library lined with books, an immense wardrobe full of clothes for the Doctor's companions, a cinema, a swimming pool, a garage, and, of vital importance, an engine room.

## Freezing Cold

When psychic pollen gets into the time rotor, a manifestation of the Doctor's psyche—the Dream Lord—appears to set the TARDIS on course for a cold sun that could freeze everything to death.

## Rival Pilot

River Song seems to understand the TARDIS better than the Doctor does. Not only does she fly and land it all by herself, but she also does so more smoothly than him. She's good, but then she's had a good teacher—a future

## All Hands on Deck

Although the TARDIS's hexagonal console was designed to have six pilots, the Doctor has been flying solo for years. But after the defeat of Davros and the Reality Bomb, the Doctor is joined by all the old faces, who help as the TARDIS tows Earth back to its rightful position

### Tardy

The Doctor has a close relationship with his TARDIS and affectionately calls her "Tardy". He doesn't like people interfering with how he flies her, but he lets River Song show him how to open her doors with a click of his fingers, not needing the key!

Spare TARDIS key concealed behind "P"

POLICE P

Phone concealed behind panel has only recently become functional

### Walking on Air

An air shell extended from the TARDIS enables Amy Pond to experience the full effect of the cosmos, floating freely and safely in open space.

POLICE TELEPHONE
FREE
FOR USE OF
PUBLIC
ADVICE & ASSISTANCE
OBTAINABLE IMMEDIATELY
OFFICERS & CARS
RESPOND TO ALL CALLS
PULL TO OPEN

The Doctor's TARDIS is stuck in the shape of a 1950s London Police Box because its chameleon circuit has been damaged

TARDIS exterior is virtually indestructible

### More Powerful than a Black Hole

The Time Lords artificially created a black hole called the Eye of Harmony. The captured energy of this black hole is the source of the TARDIS's power and is so strong that the TARDIS can escape from the gravitational pull of another black hole. The Doctor uses this tremendous power to tow Earth back to its rightful position, after it is moved to the Medusa Cascade by the Daleks.

UBLIC CALL **BOX**

A St. John Ambulance badge reflects the use of old police boxes as a point of first aid

The TARDIS can be unlocked by a key, by remote systems and even with the snap of the Doctor's fingers

# THE TARDIS

THE DOCTOR IS able to travel through time and space using a machine called the TARDIS. A triumph of Time Lord temporal engineering, TARDISes are "dimensionally transcendental" which means that the interior and exterior exist in different dimensions and they can change both their external appearance and internal layout. When the Doctor decided to flee Gallifrey and roam the universe, he stole a TARDIS awaiting servicing for a variety of malfunctions and faults. He has never been able to fully repair it, making his travels often erratic and uncontrolled.

## TARDIS FACTS

### TARDIS CORAL

TARDISes are organic vessels, grown on the Doctor's home planet of Gallifrey. A new TARDIS can be grown from a piece of coral, but this process takes many centuries.

- **The name TARDIS is an acronym of "Time And Relative Dimension In Space."**

- **The Doctor's TARDIS is a Type 40TT Capsule, considered obsolete by the Time Lords. There were originally 305 registered Type 40 TARDISes.**

- **The TARDIS has a "chameleon circuit," which is supposed to change its external appearance to blend in with its surroundings, wherever it lands.**

- **The TARDIS is able to use its telepathic circuits to translate almost any language for the benefit of its occupants.**

- **The exterior shell of the TARDIS seems to weigh no more than an ordinary police box: it can be picked up and moved with suitable machinery.**

# TARDIS Controls

The central console contains all the controls needed to fly the TARDIS. It is here that the Doctor sets the coordinates that determine the time and place of the TARDIS's materialization.

This multi-purpose monitor is a window to the outside world. Its live feed shows what's going on beyond the TARDIS and displays statistical data.

After damage from regeneration energy, the TARDIS reconfigures itself to a different template. The functions—like this atom accelerator—are the same, but they have all-new controls.

**HELM**

Time rotor handbrake • Eye piece • Steering mechanism

**ELEVENTH DOCTOR'S CONSOLE**

Time & space forward/back control

**NAVIGATION PANEL**

Locking down mechanism

**MECHANICAL PANEL**

Atom accelerator

Gyroscopic stabilizer

Directional pointer

Engine release lever

Cooling systems

Quantum foam manipulators

Sump flush

Organic diagnostic

Fabricated dispenser

Bunsen burner

**DIAGNOSTIC PANEL**

**FABRICATION PANEL**

Water dispenser

Materialize/ dematerialize fabrication

Digital communicator • Analog telephone • Scanner/ typewriter • Voice recorder

**COMMUNICATIONS PANEL**

## Cloister Bell

The cloister bell rings if the TARDIS, or the universe itself, is in dire peril. It begins to sound when Rose gives the Doctor her "Bad Wolf" message—code for "the end of the universe" and when the exploding time energy is wiping out the existence of time.

# KEY FOR THE TWELFTH DOCTOR'S TARDIS

1   Guard rail provides something safe to hold onto during bumpy flights.

2   Away from Gallifrey, the Doctor furnishes his TARDIS with oddments picked up on his travels.

3   Book-lined shelves and armchairs lend a cozy feel to the TARDIS's console room.

4   Secondary navigation panel.

5   The Doctor's professed love of "round things" may have influenced the newest design.

6   Hexagonal console shape is Gallifreyan. When "refreshed," previous versions of the "desktop" are archived in the TARDIS.

7   Access beneath the flooring allows the Doctor to make repairs to the underpanels of the console.

8   TARDIS coordinates can be fixed by entering them here.

9   The time rotor on the central column rises and falls when the TARDIS is in flight.

10  The TARIDS's telepathic cicuits extend the Doctor's Time Lord gift of languages to those in its vicinity, as long as the Doctor's brain is functioning fully.

11  One of two monitors for surveying the exterior of the TARDIS.

12  Stairs lead up to the upper level of the console room.

13  Pathways lead deeper into the TARDIS, and also back to the blue police box doors.

# SONIC SCREWDRIVERS

THE STANDARD TOOLKIT in a TARDIS contains equipment needed to tune and repair the ship. One of the most useful tools, the sonic screwdriver, uses variously focused soundwaves to make repairs where human hands cannot reach. As well as turning screws, it can open locks, operate and repair ship systems remotely and take many kinds of readings and scans.

## Time Technology

Sonic screwdrivers are a common Time Lord device. In fact, the Doctor has a number of them onboard the TARDIS, though he usually favors one particular unit. To a Time Lord, their technology is simple: if need be, the Doctor could build himself a new one from scratch in almost no time.

Although the sonic screwdriver is made from the most advanced Time Lord materials and technology, it still can't break deadlock seals or override the protocols on the *Byzantium* ship, which are being controlled by the Weeping Angels.

High-kinetic sonic waves can open almost all kinds of mechanical or electronic locks.

A reversed mode can also seal locks—useful when trying to keep an alien werewolf at bay.

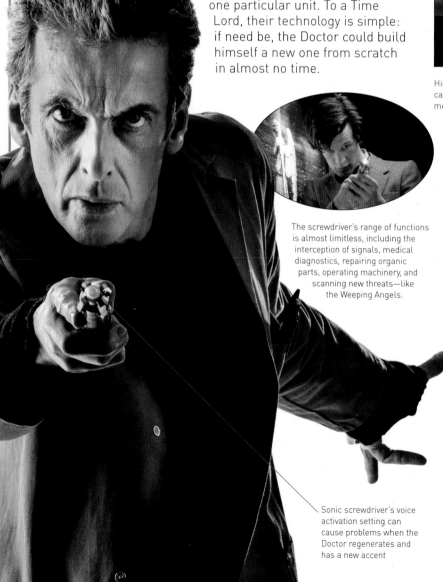

The screwdriver's range of functions is almost limitless, including the interception of signals, medical diagnostics, repairing organic parts, operating machinery, and scanning new threats—like the Weeping Angels.

Sonic screwdriver's voice activation setting can cause problems when the Doctor regenerates and has a new accent

### THE WAR DOCTOR'S SONIC SCREWDRIVER

Extendable diode

A simpler design in comparison with later models, the War Doctor's sonic was built first and foremost to be portable and functional. The outer casing might look different, but the internal sonic mechanism is the same as inside the Eleventh Doctor's casing hundreds of years later. In that amount of time, the War Doctor can start a calculation to break a material previously untouchable by sonic: wood!

In the mysterious Library, the Doctor meets River Song. Although she knows him well, for him this is their first meeting. The fact that she has an advanced sonic screwdriver, given to her in the future by the Doctor, is a sign of their strong friendship.

When the War Doctor meets future incarnations of himelf wielding sonic screwdrivers like weapons, he is most alarmed. The key to the purpose of the Doctor's handiest gadget is in its name: it's a screwdriver, designed to fix things, not attack people.

Sonic screwdrivers can remotely detonate explosives, such as bombs, and activate missiles. At a certain power setting, it can even blast a door clean off its hinges.

The beam from a sonic screwdriver can interact at a molecular level with another object, for example to "cut" a rope by unraveling the individual fibers at a particular point. It can also produce a high-energy beam capable of generating heat in order to burn or slice through many kinds of material.

# Screwdriver Operation

Sonic screwdrivers contain Gallifreyan circuitry, allowing their operator to switch between different functions using slight adjustments to the exterior casing. However, the device must be directed toward its object for maximum effectiveness. The Doctor keeps the tool on him for as long as its power cells allow between recharges.

THE ELEVENTH AND TWELFTH DOCTORS' SONIC SCREWDRIVER

Easy-grip handle

Retractable casing

Thermal insulation casing

Cooling cells

Charging cells

Primary emitter cluster

Central emitter cluster

Bracing coil

Function drums

Red button under hinged casing

Wave prism (surrounded by micro stabiliser fields)

Acoustic accelerators

Cooling cells

Primary emitter cluster

Anechoic chamber

Resonator cage

Secondary emitter cluster

# Earlier Sonic

This previous version of the sonic proved itself invaluable, getting the Doctor and his friends out of danger time after time. It was finally destroyed when the Eleventh Doctor used it to activate everything around him, hoping the Atraxi would notice the alien technology as they hunted for Prisoner Zero. As a result the outer casing burned to a crisp.

Fragile housing cracked through use

THE NINTH AND TENTH DOCTORS' SONIC SCREWDRIVER

# TOOLS OF THE TRADE

**I**N ADDITION TO his trusty sonic screwdriver, the Doctor has many devices to make life easier for him and his friends. His capacious pockets often produce a piece of technology that is just the thing for defeating a monster, but the Doctor also uses his high-tech knowledge to improvize weapons or handy gadgets. These are just a few of the things he has made use of in his travels.

Glass tube is immune to the effects of antiplastic

Page is blank until psychically activated to present an image

## Psychic Paper

Psychic paper appears blank but projects a low-level telepathic field, causing the viewer to see whatever they expect to see—such as an invitation or security pass—although it may also reflect what the holder is thinking. The Face of Boe and River Song contact the Doctor for help via his paper, and he has used it to gain entry to many secure places, such as Adipose Industries and Ood Operations. However, its use is limited: geniuses and individuals with psychic training are not fooled by the paper's trickery.

Rust inhibits functionality

Wires can be plugged into TARDIS console

Head patched with spare parts from the TARDIS

## Antiplastic

Antiplastic is a liquid that breaks down plastic into its component molecules on contact. This makes it a useful weapon against creatures made of living plastic, such as the Nestene Consciousness, who consider possession of the liquid to be a declaration of war.

## Handles the Cyberhead

Originally part of a fully functioning Cyberman, but wiped of all his destructive protocols, this robotic head, nicknamed "Handles" by the Doctor, obeys voice commands and also answers questions and attempts primitive conversations. While on Trenzalore, fighting for the town Christmas, Handles is the Doctor's only constant companion. When, corroded and battle-worn after hundreds of years' usage, he finally shuts down, his loss reduces the Doctor to tears.

## Lammersteen Scanner

The Doctor builds this bizarre contraption when he is unable to use Time Lord technology in case it discloses his presence to whatever is living above Craig Owens' flat. Based upon the non-technological engineering of Lammersteen, it scans the time interference that is preventing the TARDIS from materializing. He discovers that the flat upstairs is not a flat but a stranded spaceship.

Parabolic temporal wave shield protects scanner from outside interference

Vortex energy spikes send an alarm if the scanner is detected

Lateral balance stabilizer ensures structure will not collapse

Directional zig-zag plotter couplings provide space-time data

Luminosity discharges unused energy as light

External scanner antenna is a back-up alarm

Continuous motion energy matrix maintains power

Heat exchange conductor creates scanner's spin

Handle for sturdy grip

Activation switch makes clamp stick to surface

Base attaches to any kind of object

## Magna-Clamp

Alien magna-clamps, discovered on Earth by Torchwood operatives, cancel the mass of any object they are attached to, rendering anything up to the weight of two tons virtually weightless. They form an unbreakable bond with any surface, which the Doctor and Rose find useful when they want to avoid being pulled into the Void, while every Dalek and Cyberman is sucked in.

## Visual Recognition Device

Like much Time Lord technology, this complex gadget looks simple. When a person or creature is placed before it, the mirror displays the name of its species and planet of origin. The Doctor uses it to find out more about the mysterious Krafayis creatures that are picked up on the machine's screen, even though they are normally invisible to the human eye.

Mirror

Internal power supply

Strap for carrying or wearing the device

A present to the Doctor from one of his godmothers, the visual recognition device helps the Doctor, Amy, and the artist Vincent van Gogh when a Krafayis is loose in a French village in 1890.

Power source

## Gravity Globe

Wide beams of light are easily supplied by these portable gravity globes. Defying gravity, they float high in the air and are, as such, very useful in large enclosed spaces. The Doctor uses one to explore the dark Weeping Angel-infested caves of Aplan Mortarium.

## PATHOGENESIS DETECTOR

The Doctor improvises this pathogenesis detector from an ordinary electricity plug, some light bulbs, and basic TARDIS technology. It tracks creatures and flashes red whenever alien life forms, such as Adipose, are nearby.

This power source is a core component of cyborgs (part-robotic, part-biological creatures). It can also be used to create a strong electromagnetic pulse that will scramble the circuits of any robot in the vicinity.

## ELECTROMAGNETIC POWER SOURCE

Power-level display

Coral from the organic body of the TARDIS

Rotating probes

Bulb glows red in presence of suspicious findings

Bell makes satisfying "ding" sound

Antenna for scouring landscape for alien DNA

## DNA Device

Known by the Doctor as the "machine that goes ding," this homemade device supposedly lights up in the presence of aliens who are not in their natural form. Intended to detect shape-shifting Zygon DNA, it is instead distracted by innocent rabbits and horses. The Doctor claims it can also microwave frozen dinners and download comics from the future.

## Tribophysical Waveform Macro-kinetic Extrapolator

This extrapolator can be used as a form of transport, as it acts as a pan-dimensional surfboard, shielding its user in a force field and then riding energy waves to a preset destination. It can be misused to lock onto another's energy source and take their power. Integrated into the TARDIS, it emits a force field that helps the ship resist external forces exerted upon it, and it also speeds up the TARDIS refueling process.

# TIME LORDS

LONG AGO, THE DOCTOR'S people, the Time Lords, were a great civilization. They built an advanced society on their planet, Gallifrey, where they thrived for millions of years. However, they were corrupted by the fighting of the Great Time War and their values became twisted—so much so that they posed a threat to the entire universe, and even to time itself.

Steely gaze

Space where White Point Star once sat

Staff of office

Two hearts, as with all Time Lords

## The Ultimate Sanction

After the Daleks discovered that the Time Lords had tried to tamper with history to prevent their creation, they declared war and the conflict called the last Great Time War began. Driven to ensure their survival at any cost, the High Council planned the Ultimate Sanction: to destroy the universe and all of time. They would then evolve into a higher consciousness to exist outside of time.

## High Council Lord President

As the legendary founder of Time Lord society, Rassilon was a revered hero to many of his people. However, by the end of the Time War, the power he exercises as Lord President has corrupted him and he has become obsessed with avoiding death at all costs. Having made a link with rogue Time Lord the Master, Rassilon removes a White Point Star from his staff and sends it to Earth, creating a psychic link that will allow Gallifrey to escape the Time War.

The Great Time War is time-locked, so the events cannot by changed with time travel. On what will be the last day of the war, the trapped High Council are aware of their imminent destruction. They seek approval for use of the Ultimate Sanction to escape their demise.

Gloved hand shoots electricity bolts

Interior pockets contain Time Lord devices

RASSILON

Before all versions of the Doctors come together to save Gallifrey, the Time Lords plan to use Earth as the key to their escape. Despite his loneliness, the Doctor is unable to rejoice in the return of his people. He knows he must destroy them all over again. It's a heart-breaking decision, but they are still set on the Ultimate Sanction, which he cannot allow. The Doctor shoots the White Point Star, severing the link between Gallifrey and Earth, and returning the Time Lords, led by Rassilon, to the last days of the Time War.

## Gallifrey

The Time Lords come from Gallifrey, a planet located in the constellation of Kasterborous, some 29,000 light years from Earth. Until its destruction in the Great Time War, Gallifrey is a divided world. The Time Lords dwell in vast citadels enclosed in mighty glass domes, while the Outsiders, the outcasts of Gallifreyan society, lead tribal lives in the wilderness beyond the cities.

Gallifrey's Capitol is the seat of Time Lord power. It houses the Academies of Learning, the time-monitoring facilities, the controls for the impenetrable forcefield that protects the planet and the Eye of Harmony—the artificial black hole that provided the energy needed for time travel.

Gallifrey's second city, Arcadia, is supposedly the safest place on the planet—protected by 400 sky trenches. However, on the last day of the Time War, the Daleks blast their way through Arcadia's defenses and the city's destruction is captured forever in a 3D painting.

The Doctor remembers Gallifrey as a beautiful planet. Underneath its burnt orange sky was a world of endless snow-capped mountains, with silver-leafed trees and plains of red grass. However, by the end of the Time War, the planet has been ravaged by the Daleks.

## The War Council

Led by the military General, the Time Lord War Council was established to deal directly with the Dalek assault on Gallifrey. From their meetings within Gallifrey's Capitol War Room, the War Council rejects the authority of the High Council and President Rassilon in a last-ditch attempt to save Gallifrey.

Rich red and purple colourings of Council

COUNCIL MEMBER

The Seal of Rassilon

Lightweight protective armor

Different ceremonial robes and collar from the High Council

ANDROGAR

THE GENERAL

## THE MOMENT

Otherwise known as the "Galaxy Eater," the Moment is the most destructive weapon in all of creation and feared even by the Time Lords themselves. Classed as a forbidden weapon, it is kept securely in Gallifrey's time vaults—until it is stolen by the War Doctor, who intends to use it to destroy the Time Lords and the Daleks, and so end the war.

Gallifreyan markings

Intricately carved cogs and wheels

Big red button in the shape of a glowing jewel

The Moment's basic form is a wooden box full of whirring gears, but when the War Doctor complains about the lack of an activating button, it morphs into a shape that matches his expectations.

Expanded metal form

Surface can become red hot when activated

## Gallifrey Stands

With the Dalek firepower increasing, the General commands the Doctor to carry out his alternative plan to save Gallifrey, realizing that they have no other options. All thirteen of the Doctor's incarnations come together to freeze Gallifrey in a single moment in time, preserving it in a parallel pocket universe.

## The Moment's Conscience

The Moment is such a sophisticated device that it actually became sentient and developed a conscience. When the War Doctor tries to use it, the Moment's interface activates in the form of Bad Wolf Rose Tyler and attempts to convince him not to commit genocide.

# RIVER SONG

ARCHEOLOGIST-FOR-HIRE River Song is a formidable woman. Exceptionally brave and fiercely loyal, she is a good ally to have, although the Doctor finds her reckless at times. The Doctor and River have always met at different points in their time streams, which makes for a complicated relationship. The Doctor is wary of her because of this, but he accepts that their lives are inextricably linked.

## Muddled time streams

River and the Doctor are always meeting in the wrong order because her past is his future. Her last meeting with the Doctor is his first. On the Library world, she courageously sacrifices herself to save the Doctor, because she knows how important he is to the future.

Scanner and communicator for locating life forms and assessing terrain

Leather holster and spare pockets

Strap secures holster for gun

Serial number

Energy bolt firer

Light-weight material

### RIVER'S PISTOL

Unsentimental River has no qualms about using weapons—once even shooting dead a Dalek in the National Museum.

## Extraordinary Explorer

River Song is no ordinary professor of archeology. She is highly experienced in her field and has led many treacherous expeditions. Her outfits always hide an array of gadgets, such as hallucinogenic lipstick and disarming weapons disguised as earrings, and she has proved herself to be a skilled gun-fighter, especially against the Daleks and the Silents. She has a particular fascination for the Weeping Angels—beings she has investigated and fought several times.

### HOME BOX

A Home Box records data onboard a spacecraft, similar to the black box on a plane. The one River uses to reach the Doctor is from the starliner *Byzantium*. When the Doctor finds it, it is 12,000 years old and kept as a museum exhibit.

Message reads, "Hello, sweetie!"

Old High Gallifreyan writing

River uses the *Byzantium*'s Home Box to send a message to the Doctor when she is in urgent need of his help. She carves her coordinates into the metal and then jumps out of the ship into space, confident that the TARDIS will appear in time. River has such faith in the Doctor that she's prepared to stake her life on it.

## SQUARENESS GUN

This gun could be the same one used by Captain Jack Harkness. River has a habit of borrowing what appear to be his belongings—including a vortex manipulator.

Handle contains short-life dark matter battery

Switch sets function: Sonic Cannon, Blaster, or Disruptor

Sonic waves form pulsing squares of blue light that can cut through walls

## RIVER SONG FACTS

- River is thought to be the only person who knows the Doctor's real name.
- River marries the Doctor in an alternative timeline, but the pair still treat each other as husband and wife after time is rewritten.
- River has intimate knowledge of Time Lords: she can write in Old High Gallifreyan, the lost language of the Time Lords.
- River once saved the Doctor's life by giving him all of her remaining regenerations.
- Although River finally dies on the Library world, her data ghost is preserved in its computer systems, allowing her to appear as a projection to the Doctor on Trenzalore.

## SONIC SCREWDRIVER

Wave amplifiers

Master function key houses neural relay

Setting dials

Enhanced emitter lens is superior to the Tenth Doctor's screwdriver

TARDIS remote return

User recognition ring

The Doctor giving River one of his sonic screwdrivers is a sign of his great respect for her.

## DIARY OF SPOILERS

River refuses to reveal any "spoilers" about the Doctor's future, and uses her diary to keep track of their time streams. He has a matching diary monitoring events from his own point of view. To allow her to recognize the Doctor, her diary contains pictures of all his different faces.

Cover resembles the TARDIS

Confident and used to getting her own way, River treats the Doctor with a familiarity that no one else would presume to have. She enjoys showing off, and revels in the fact that she can fly the TARDIS better than he can. He isn't used to finding himself in such a position, but they still make a good team.

## Trained Killer

As an adult, River Song is again captured by the Silence. She is forced into an automated Apollo spacesuit and placed under Lake Silencio in Utah to wait for the Doctor. Although the Doctor's death is meant to be a fixed point in time, River's affection for the man she loves gets in the way. She refuses to shoot him and time itself begins to unravel.

## Melody Pond

River is actually Amy and Rory's daughter, born Melody Pond, and, thanks to the influence of the time vortex, with the Time Lord ability to regenerate. She discovers this power for the first time in 1970s New York after escaping from her kidnappers the Silence – who intended to raise her to become the Doctor's assassin.

Frail body hides inhuman strength

Concealed pistol

MELS

After traveling to England, Melody eventually grows up alongside her parents, who nickname her "Mels," although they have no idea who she really is. Her identity is fully revealed when she regenerates into the familiar form of River Song in front of her astonished parents.

Although she didn't kill the Doctor at Lake Silencio, River still serves a prison sentence at the Stormcage Containment Facility in order to convince the Silence that their target is finally dead. She is eventually released after the Doctor erases records of himself from every database in the universe.

# CLARA OSWALD

FOR A LONG TIME, Clara is an inexplicable mystery to the Doctor, since he can't fathom how the same person can possibly exist at different points in time and space. He initially meets Oswin Oswald on the Daleks' asylum planet before an encounter with Clara Oswald—a barmaid-and-governess from Victorian times. By the time he meets the original modern-day Clara, he becomes obsessed with solving the mystery of his "impossible girl" once and for all.

Comfortable clothes suitable for teaching at school or a sudden, unplanned adventure

Stylish leather skirt

## Adapting to Change

Having developed a special bond with the Eleventh Doctor, Clara is shocked when he regenerates into a brand new body. She finds it difficult relating to a version of her friend who not only looks radically different, but who also seems more alien and distant. Over time, however, she learns to get to know the Doctor all over again and warms to his new persona.

When the Great Intelligence enters the Doctor's time stream in an attempt to rewrite his life, Clara realzes that it's her destiny to reverse its baleful influence. She bravely enters the time tunnel herself and is scattered into a million different fragments, each aspect of herself determined to save the Doctor at different points in time and space.

## CLARA OSWALD FACTS

🔖 At some point, each version of Clara says the same enigmatic phrase to the Doctor: "Run, you clever boy, and remember me."

🔖 Adventurous Clara has become used to thrills with the Doctor and so enjoys riding her motorcycle to work every day.

🔖 One of Clara's splintered selves ends up on Gallifrey where she persuades the First Doctor to take a different TARDIS from the one that he intended to steal.

🔖 Clara is determined to one day make the perfect soufflé, although most of her attempts seem to go badly wrong.

## A Loyal Friend

Clara is smart, witty, and headstrong—admirable qualities shared by the many different versions of herself. The perfect companion to the Doctor, she is brave and resourceful and willing to take the lead, even in the most terrifying of situations. For all her strength of character, though, she is never afraid to allow her caring side to shine through. She brings hope to the Doctor when he is scared that there might be none left for him, and sees the goodness in him that he cannot.

## CLARA'S COPY OF *101 PLACES TO SEE*

Embossed cover worn with age and use

Clara's handwriting records her age

The modern-day version of Clara longs to travel the world, and one of her most treasured childhood possessions is a book full of wonderful places to visit. Each birthday, Clara crosses out her previous age and writes in the new one on the inside page.

## Dalek Oswald

A fast and funny junior entertainment officer aboard the starship *Alaska*, Oswin Oswald believes she has survived alone on the Daleks' asylum world for a whole year. In reality, she has subconsciously created a dream-world for herself in order to block out the appalling truth—that she's actually been turned from a human into a Dalek.

## Victorian Clara

The Victorian version of Clara is a feisty and fearless girl who leads a secret double life, alternating between jobs as a posh governess and down-to-earth barmaid. She's curious about the Doctor and his time machine, but, tragically, her time with him is cut short when she is killed by the Great Intelligence's sentient ice governess.

Clara's book of places to see originally belonged to her mom, Ellie, who tragically died when Clara was only a teenager. Clara regards the book as a precious object as a result.

Following the death of Victorian Clara, an obsessed Doctor withdraws to a place of solitude and paints a striking portrait of her. He hopes it will inspire him to unravel the perplexing mystery of her existence.

Some time after quitting her job as a nanny, Clara becomes an English teacher at Coal Hill—the same school that the Doctor's granddaughter Susan once studied at. Alongside the Doctor, "Miss Oswald" ends up defending Coal Hill against a rampaging alien war machine.

## The Maitland Family

Expression displays cheerful demeanor

When the Doctor first meets modern-day Clara, she's working as a nanny for the Maitland family. She intended to stay with them for just a week, but when Artie and Angie's mother died, their grief strikes a chord with her and she decides to stay on and look after the family.

Arms crossed in stubborn teenager pose

ARTIE MAITLAND

ANGIE MAITLAND

Having found photographs of Clara on the Internet, Archie and Angie work out that their nanny is a time-traveler. They playfully threaten to reveal her secret unless she agrees to take them on trip in the Doctor's TARDIS.

# DANNY PINK

A MATH TEACHER at Coal Hill School, Danny Pink is a man haunted by his military past, despite all the good work he did during his time as a soldier. While he is brave, loyal, and principled, Danny can also be shy and nervous around others, and it takes him time to overcome his awkwardness with colleague Clara. When he, at last, becomes close to her, he can't help getting caught up in her incredible adventures with the Doctor, and soon discovers that his life has changed forever.

## Sensitive Subject

Danny's outwardly tough persona belies his true feelings. He finds it difficult to talk about his army days, particularly when questioned about the lives he took during active service. He believes that people often misunderstand the life of a soldier, and jump to wrong conclusions about the kind of man they think he is.

Short military haircut

Habitual standing-to-attention stance

Formal clothes adhere to dress code for teaching at Coal Hill

Pajamas provided by care home

### RUPERT PINK

Danny grew up in a children's home in Gloucester in the 1990s. Even as a little boy, he hated his real name, Rupert, and decided he wanted to change it when he got older. When the Doctor connects Clara to the TARDIS's telepathic circuits, she is subconsciously thinking about Danny's past and accidentally takes the time machine back to Rupert's time zone, where the pair of them help the lonely young boy deal with an unseen alien terror lurking in his bedroom.

## The Trials of Teaching

As a new teacher at Coal Hill School, Danny finds it a challenge getting along with some of his pupils, especially when they start probing him for details of his life as a soldier. However, he feels on surer ground when he's back in military mode, barking out orders as the head of the Coal Hill Cadet Squad.

## Colonel Orson Pink

Hailing from a hundred years in Earth's future, Colonel Orson Pink was the first man on the planet to travel in time, after being inspired by the incredible stories of one of his great grandparents. Orson's pioneering exploits went disastrously wrong, however. He was meant to travel forward only a few days, but somehow overshot and ended up stranded on a wilderness world—becoming the last man standing at the very end of the universe.

Sanctuary Base 6 logo

Airtight helmet

Protective orange spacesuit from the Doctor's TARDIS wardrobe

Socket for attaching oxygen tube

Danny has an uneasy relationship with the Doctor to begin with, since the Time Lord reminds him of some of the hardened officers he served under in the army. Danny is wary of how the Doctor keeps pushing Clara to do things that put her life in danger, and he can't help but feel protective toward her.

When Coal Hill School is threatened by a deadly Skovox Blitzer, Danny is lucky to escape the ensuing battle with his life. First, he is shot at by the Blitzer's laser cannon, then almost dragged into a whirling time vortex opened up by the Doctor as means of disposing of the alien war machine.

## Blossoming Romance

Although they're attracted to one another, Danny and Clara have something of a tempestuous relationship. Danny is sensitive to Clara's spiky humor and the pair seem to misunderstand each other at almost every turn. Her strange and regular disappearances with the Doctor don't help him to trust her. However, when Clara learns more about Danny's past and possible future, she warms to him much more and the pair gradually form a close relationship.

# AMY POND

**B**RAVE, BOLD, AND DECISIVE, Amy is a good traveling companion for the Doctor. She is not afraid of dangerous situations, speaking her mind or even challenging her Time Lord best friend. Her whole life changed when she first met the Doctor when she was seven years old. Although a TARDIS malfunction meant that she had to wait 12 years before seeing him again, she's never looked back since!

Amy's clothes reveal her great sense of style

## Gutsy Pond!

Confident and fearless, Amy is ready to deal with anything that comes her way. But a small part of her is still the vulnerable child who was abandoned, first by her parents and then by the Doctor. When he finally returns, she is all grown up, but it takes her a while to forgive him. After the Doctor resets the universe, time is rewritten, meaning Amy's parents never went away.

Wedding ring worn with pride

## Amy and her Boys

Amy has had the Doctor on a pedestal since she was a child, but has pragmatically settled with Rory. When the Doctor returns and she travels in the TARDIS, it turns her head and she starts doubting her relationship with Rory. However, adventures eventually reveal the Doctor's fallibility and Rory's strength. She comes to happily take Rory as her husband. But far from settling down, they leave their wedding party to return to the TARDIS with the Doctor.

Amy is not daunted by the famous or powerful people she meets as a result of traveling with the Doctor. She doesn't hesitate to take charge of formidable prime minister Winston Churchill when the Daleks threaten Earth. He is impressed with her bravery and leadership, and wishes he had more people like her in his war effort against the Nazis.

## AMY POND FACTS

- **Amelia Jessica Pond changes her name to Amy after the Doctor says that Amelia sounds like something from a fairy tale.**

- **Amy's parents are Tabetha and Augustus, but she is raised by her Aunt Sharon when her parents are swallowed by a crack in time.**

- **Amy moved to Leadworth, England from Inverness, Scotland when she was young, but never lost her Scottish accent.**

- **In a break from traveling with the Doctor, Amy becomes a model, but quits when she realizes it is damaging her relationship with Rory. She then turns to travel writing.**

Artist Vincent van Gogh is an unusual character. An outcast in his village, people find him very difficult. Amy isn't intimidated and uses her charms to diffuse a tense situation and win him over. He loves her frankness and passion for life.

Amy and the Doctor settle into a comfortable friendship. Her insight brings new perspectives to the Doctor, and he helps her to be brave in the face of many fearsome aliens and enemies. In quiet moments, they bicker about the most ordinary things—such as his habit of reading books backwards and his dislike of her reading glasses.

The Doctor is distraught when Amy and Rory become stuck back in time by the Weeping Angels. He learns to travel without them, but at his moment of regeneration, he imagines both a young Amelia and grown-up Amy returning to him, comforting him by calling him "Raggedy Man" once again.

Newborn Melody Pond, wrapped in a blanket

Sterile hospital clothes

# Mother of Melody

Amy's darkest hour comes when the Order of the Silence steals her and Rory's baby to brainwash and use as a weapon against the Doctor. Motherhood is a big change for independent Amy Pond, and losing her newborn is a difficult loss to deal with.

Amy and Rory are astonished when they discover the woman they have traveled with on several occasions, River Song, is in fact their daughter Melody Pond! Having absorbed energies from the TARDIS, she was born with the ability to regenerate like a Time Lord—meaning their child was not lost to them, as they feared, after all.

## PAPIER-MÂCHÉ DOLLS

Blue shirt resembles the one worn by the Doctor when he appeared in Amy's garden

To while away her loneliness and convince herself that she wasn't imagining everything, Amy made puppets of the Doctor and put on shows.

AMELIA'S DRAWINGS

Woolly hat for autumn

Smiley face carved by Amelia, like her mother used to do

## SMILEY APPLE

When the Doctor returns, he convinces Amy he has been gone only for a few minutes because the carved apple she gave him is still fresh.

The crashed TARDIS in Amy's garden

# Amelia Pond

Little Amy, called by her full name Amelia, is the girl who waits a long time for the Doctor. He needs to stabilize the TARDIS and promises he'll be back in five minutes. But the engines phase and he doesn't come back for 12 years. Amelia grows up unable to convince anyone that the Doctor is real, including four psychiatrists. She grows up feeling abandoned and set apart from anyone else, but she never gives up her dream of time travel.

Warm clothes, ready for adventures with the Doctor

Very little scares Amelia, not even an alien man in a box falling from the sky in the middle of the night.

Eager to join the Doctor in the TARDIS, determined Amelia packs her suitcase for traveling the stars.

# RORY WILLIAMS

RORY WILLIAMS is a straightforward guy, content with his life in sleepy Leadworth, England, so long as he is with Amy Pond, the love of his life. They have known each other since childhood, but he has always felt second-best to Amy's spaceman Doctor. Rory is astounded to discover that the Doctor is real, and he is initially worried: a flesh-and-blood rival is a more serious threat than an imaginary friend.

Pointy nose subject of teasing by the Doctor

Tougher stance result of confidence developed from adventures in TARDIS

Life with the Doctor is dazzling and can blind people to the things that are important. The Doctor senses that Amy has drifted too far from Rory. So he brings Rory along for a trip in the TARDIS so the couple can reconnect. Rory is surprised how distant Amy seems when he'd seen her only a few hours earlier. For her, she's not even sure how long it's been since she saw him.

## Nurse Rory

Compassionate Rory makes a good nurse, but he would have preferred to have been a doctor. He isn't very forceful and struggles to stand up to people who intimidate him, like hospital consultants or even self-assured Amy. But when it really matters, Rory proves that he is brave and has the strength to stand up to anything to protect those he loves.

Amy feels torn between the exciting Doctor and ordinary Rory. However, events in a dream sequence help her realize that Rory is the one for her. In the dream, he is killed by alien Eknodines and she kills herself by crashing an RV because she'd rather die than live without him.

### RORY'S HOSPITAL PASS

Rory's work pass gives him and Amy access to Leadworth Hospital when they are tracking Prisoner Zero to stop the Atraxi from destroying Earth.

Pass shows that Rory works in the ER

RLH Royal Leadworth Hospital
RORY WILLIAMS
EMERGENCY UNIT
039421

## Rory and the Doctor

Rory and the Doctor do not hit it off when they first meet. However, when Rory travels in the TARDIS, he witnesses first hand the appeal of the Doctor. The Doctor shows him things he could never have imagined before, and gives him renewed faith in the universe.

## Rory's Dad

Brian Williams never truly bonded with his son Rory until they adventure together aboard the TARDIS. Father and son discover their shared piloting skills when they command a Silurian Ark and fight off dinosaurs together.

Rory has always known that he was meant to be with Amy forever. When he is sent back in time by a Weeping Angel, he thinks he will never see his beloved wife again. But Amy has grown to realize that her love for Rory is forever too. Even knowing she will never be able to see the Doctor again, Amy chooses to join Rory in the past, where they live the rest of their lives together.

### RORY AND AMY'S GRAVESTONE

IN LOVING MEMORY
RORY ARTHUR WILLIAMS
AGED 82

AND HIS LOVING WIFE
AMELIA WILLIAMS
AGED 87

Rory and Amy's humble gravestone sits in a New York cemetery. It is initially engraved with just Rory's name, but when Amy goes back in time to be with her husband, her name appears on the gravestone too. Its simple wording reveals that they lived on into their eighties together.

Unassuming granite gravestone

## Nestene Rory

In an alternative timeline, Rory is consumed by energy from the cracks in the universe and ceases to exist. However, in 102CE, he appears as a Roman centurion. He looks like Rory and believes he is Rory, but he is in fact an Auton: a Nestene duplicate retrieved from Amy's memories. He doesn't age and can live indefinitely, but he is not immortal. His plastic body cannot heal, so he must keep away from heat and radio signals.

Skin looks human but has slight plastic sheen

Armor of a Roman Centurion

Amy and Rory have only just rekindled their relationship when Rory succumbs to Nestene control. He is desperate to be human, but he cannot stop himself from shooting Amy. In order to keep her alive, the Doctor encloses Amy in the stasis-locked Pandorica until he can revive her.

Rory displays his dedication to Amy by guarding her in the Pandorica Box for 2,000 years. He becomes part of the Pandorica legend as the mystery figure "the Lone Centurion." He is written about by Emperor Hadrian, and Isaac Newton and Samuel Pepys call him a friend. The story of the Lone Centurion ends with him carrying the Box from a burning warehouse during the Blitz. However, Rory's story continues: he is by the Pandorica to be reunited with Amy when she is revived in 2010, and is ready to use his Auton weapon to protect her and the Doctor.

# LEADWORTH

THE QUAINT ENGLISH village of Leadworth in rural Gloucestershire, England, is home to Amy Pond and Rory Williams. With little more than a church, a pub, a post office, a fire station, and a duck pond, the village is not vibrant, but it does have a strong sense of neighborliness. Leadworth is the last place you would expect anything out of the ordinary to happen.

Life in the village might seem idyllic, but it is actually the focus of a terrifying alien threat. A dangerous alien, called Prisoner Zero, has escaped imprisonment by the Atraxi and is hiding in Leadworth and causing local people to fall into comas. In an attempt to recapture the alien, the Atraxi threaten to incinerate Earth.

## Amy's House

Strange disturbances around a crack in space and time bring the TARDIS to this house, where Amy Pond lives with her aunt. The Doctor discovers that Amy is no ordinary girl: her house has too many rooms and the crack in her wall has been pouring the power of the universe through her dreams.

Memorial to those from the Leadworth area who died in the two World Wars

To Leadworth Hospital

Amy doesn't remember ever seeing any ducks on the duck pond

Pub is the heart of village life and where Rory's bachelor party is interrupted by the Doctor

## Leadworth Hospital

Royal Leadworth Hospital, on the outskirts of town, is where Rory works as a nurse. The hospital is also the focus of the alien Prisoner Zero, when it is on the run from the Atraxi. The multi-form creates psychic links with coma patients and takes on their appearances to disguise itself as human.

Leadworth Church is where Amy and Rory finally say "I do"

To Amy's house

Ruins are all that remain of Leadworth House

Jeff Angelo's house is where the Doctor saves the world from the Atraxi

## Upper Leadworth

The Dream Lord, an incarnation of the Doctor's dark psyche, creates a false reality in Upper Leadworth, a place that time forgot. Five years in the future, Rory and Amy have settled down. Rory has everything he ever wanted: Amy, a home, a baby on the way, and a career as a respected doctor. However, Amy feels trapped after the excitement of traveling with the Doctor and is glad to see him return, even if it does spell danger.

## Eknodines

The Dream Lord's version of Leadworth has been invaded by Eknodines, who are aliens fleeing their home world. On Earth, they take over the bodies of elderly human hosts. Angered at having been driven from their home, they want to destroy other races. The Eknodines reveal green eye-stalks from their hosts' mouths. Their tentacles spray a green cloud of lethal gas that can reduce people to dust in seconds.

# CAPTAIN JACK HARKNESS

Born in the Boeshane Peninsula, "Jack" was recruited to the Time Agency, a mysterious espionage organization, but left after it stole two years of his memory. Used to the free and easy ways of the 51st century, and blessed with natural good looks and winning ways, he put his enormous charm to work as a con man, taking the identity of a Captain Jack Harkness. He has never revealed his true name.

Stranded on Earth in 1869 after leaving Satellite 5, Jack moves to the site of Cardiff's Rift to wait for the Doctor. He is recruited by Torchwood Three. In 2000, he becomes leader and builds a team including Ianto Jones and Gwen Cooper.

Stripes for rank of Captain

## A Hidden Hero

Captain Jack surprises himself by discovering that he can be courageous and selfless. After meeting the Doctor, he leaves his criminal ways and the two become good friends. During Jack's ensuing adventures, he proves himself as a hero—one who is willing to risk his life for a noble cause.

Jack owes his immortality to Rose Tyler, who brings him back to life after he is exterminated by Daleks on Satellite 5. Rose opens the heart of the TARDIS and absorbs the Time Vortex. She gains its tremendous powers, but is unable to fully control them, causing Jack to be returned, not for one lifetime, but forever, a mistake which he proceeds to put to good use.

World War II overcoat

Microphone

Receiver

### VORTEX MANIPULATOR

Jack wears a vortex manipulator on his wrist. He uses the device to travel through time. Jack discovered this most useful of gadgets at the Time Agency. In addition to time travel, it can scan for alien technology, project simple holographics, and perform basic medical examinations.

The Face of Boe sacrifices himself to free the people of New Earth, and imparts his dying secret to the Doctor: "You Are Not Alone." This hint that the Master is living as Professor Yana at the end of the universe gives a clue to the fact that the Face of Boe has been to the far future as Captain Jack.

## The Face of Boe

What happens to an immortal who keeps aging? Jack had been a poster boy in his homeland, the Boeshane Peninsula, earning the nickname "the Face of Boe." The Doctor has met another Face of Boe—a giant alien head. Is this who Captain Jack will become after billions of years?

# DONNA NOBLE

Fiery red hair matches her fiery temper

Confident face hides self-doubt

S HE WAS A LOUDMOUTH who hated Christmas, could not point to Germany on a map, and deep down, thought she was worthless. But being with the Doctor allows long-term temp Donna to see herself in a new way. She shows she has compassion and sense, and when she saves the cosmos from Davros's Reality Bomb, Donna is the most important woman in the whole universe.

Donna missed the Sycorax invasion (hungover) and the Cybermen (scuba-diving in Spain), but she has front row seats for the Racnoss.

## Unlikely Friends

Thanks to Donna's quick temper and sharp tongue, she and the Doctor do not hit it off at first. As their relationship develops, however, Donna learns that not only is she intelligent and compassionate, but she can also do some real good in the world. Eventually, the Doctor considers Donna his best friend.

Being with Donna changes the Doctor and it turns out that without her, there would be no Doctor at all. A beetle belonging to a being known as the Trickster reveals an alternative timeline in which Donna never met the Doctor and he was killed by the Racnoss.

### TRICKSTER'S BEETLE

This giant stag beetle attaches itself firmly to a victim's back, changing her timeline and causing chaos. It can be seen only by those with psychic abilities.

Giant insectoid form

Smart suit for office work

Donna's compassion influences the Doctor. When they visit Pompeii she convinces him to save Caecilius's family, and she shares responsibility for destroying the city so that he doesn't have to bear the weight alone.

### Wilfred Mott

An amateur astronomer with an interest in aliens, Wilf adores Donna, his only grandchild, and thinks she should go with the Doctor as it is a once-in-a-lifetime opportunity to explore the stars. He has his own role to play in saving the world from the Time Lords, and the Doctor sacrifices his tenth incarnation to save him.

### Sylvia Noble

Donna's mother cannot forgive the Doctor for helping to ruin Donna's first wedding. She does not want her daughter to go away with him. Deep down, Sylvia is proud of Donna, but is not very good at showing it.

### The Doctor-Donna

Donna becomes the only person who can save the universe from Davros when she fuses with the Doctor's severed hand. This creates a human Doctor and also gives Donna the knowledge of a Time Lord—becoming the "Doctor-Donna." But a Time Lord brain is so powerful that a human host cannot survive. The Doctor must say goodbye: if Donna ever remembers him, she will die.

# ROSE TYLER

LONDON TEENAGER Rose Tyler's world is transformed the night she is attacked by possessed mannequins. A mysterious stranger called the Doctor saves her life and offers her a way out of her dull life as a shop assistant—a chance to travel across the universe. But this amazing adventure comes at a cost. Rose must leave behind her mom, Jackie, who is also her best friend, her boyfriend, Mickey, and the life she knows on Earth.

## Traveling Companion

Rose is quick witted, intelligent, and determined—assets that make her the ideal traveling companion. Overawed by life with the Doctor at first, she soon takes to time travel with gusto. Best of all, Rose has a wicked sense of humor that makes their adventures together fun.

## Parallel Rose

Rose is thrilled by her exciting life with the Doctor, whom she begins to realize she loves. But her time with him comes to a sudden end when she is sucked into a parallel world. She returns to reality in times of great need, but must always return to her parallel existence.

When she looks into the heart of the TARDIS, Rose absorbs the energy of the time vortex. It gives her great power over time and space, but starts to destroy her. The Doctor sacrifices his ninth incarnation to save her.

Discount clothes from Hendrik's department store

## A Doctor for Rose

Rose's forays into this reality often save the day, but she must still return to her parallel life. Despite their love, the Doctor cannot join her. However, his human clone version—created from his hand—can. He is just like the Doctor, except that he is Rose's own kind.

## Mickey Smith

Rose's boyfriend Mickey is jealous when Rose leaves with the Doctor, but he soon gets his chance at adventure too. When forced to rely on himself, and after facing many deadly aliens, Mickey becomes a brave freedom fighter.

## Jackie Tyler

After Pete Tyler's death, Jackie was left to raise their daughter on her own. Jackie is funny and popular, although often brash. She loves Rose and resents the Doctor for taking her away, but feels affection for him too.

# MARTHA JONES

Standard issue white medical coat

Comfortable clothes are perfect for the hectic schedule of a doctor

**C**APABLE AND INDEPENDENT, medical student Martha Jones impresses the Doctor right from the start. When the Royal Hope Hospital is transported to the moon by the rhino-headed Judoon, Martha remains calm, while all around her panic. Within hours of meeting the Doctor, she not only saves his life, but manages to save Earth too.

## Medical Student

Martha is less in awe of the Doctor than his previous companion Rose was. As a medical student, she is comfortable in the world of science, and quickly grasps the complex concepts his world revolves around. She spends much of her time feeling second best to Rose, but her actions show that she is just what the Doctor ordered.

Martha is compassionate and positive. When the warmongering Sontarans create a clone of her for their army, her clone self looks into her mind, sees all her hopes and dreams, and changes allegiance as it dies.

When the Master ravages life on Earth, Martha becomes a legend by spreading hope and telling stories of the Doctor around the world. But her success wipes out her celebrity: she is forgotten when the Master is defeated and time is reversed.

## The Jones Family

Martha learns that families and the Doctor do not mix when her family is used as pawns by the Master. She feels responsible for their suffering, and gives up time-travelling to keep mom, Francine, dad, Clive, and sister, Tish, safe from future danger.

## A United Front

With Martha's record of saving the world, it is no surprise that the Unified Intelligence Taskforce (UNIT)—the organization tasked with defending Earth—want her on their medical staff. It might look like she has become a soldier, but principled Martha is working from the inside to stop the fighting. The Doctor taught her well.

# HUMAN ALLIES

**A**S WELL AS HIS regular traveling companions, the Doctor has always relied on others to help him overcome the many alien threats to planet Earth. More often than not, his human allies are innocent bystanders caught up in the fight, while others are willing adventurers—as brave and selfless as the Doctor himself.

CRAIG OWENS

SOPHIE

Craig and his girlfriend, Sophie, have the Doctor to thank for bringing them together as a couple. They are now the mostly happy parents to a son—Alfie.

### The FBI Agent

A hard-bitten ex-Bureau agent from 1969, Canton is, at first, somewhat bemused by the Doctor and his incredible time-ship. However, he quickly grows to respect the alien Time Lord and his companions, and remains loyal to them until old age.

CANTON EVERETT DELAWARE III

### Mr. Sofa Man

An unashamed couch potato, Craig's life is turned upside down when he takes the Doctor in as a lodger. He has twice been drawn into the Doctor's investigations, and despite his desire to be left alone, now counts the Doctor as his friend.

JOHN RIDDELL

### The Arwell Family

Bereft mom Madge and curious children Cyril and Lily were facing a gloomy evacuation in the countryside during World War II. An encounter with the Doctor brings them closer together, and enables them to free an endangered race of tree creatures.

Madge's World War II pilot husband, Reg, was believed lost at sea, but thanks to Madge and the Doctor's heroics, the Arwell family is happily reunited in time for Christmas.

MADGE

CYRIL

LILY

### The Big Game Hunter

Self-professed thrill-seeker John Riddell has seen much excitement alongside the Doctor. His highlight was hunting dinosaurs on a Silurian Ark in space, an adventure that made him feel more alive than ever before.

### Ghost Hunters

In the 1970s, psychology professor Alec Palmer and his psychic assistant, Emma, are looking for a ghost called Hila Tacorian, a pioneer time traveler trapped in a pocket universe. The Doctor uses Emma's psychic powers to free the lost human.

MAJOR ALEC PALMER

EMMA GRAYLING

# TORCHWOOD

IN 1879, QUEEN VICTORIA VISITED Torchwood House in Scotland, where she met the Doctor and discovered the existence of aliens. Determined that the British Empire would be ready for its next extraterrestrial visitors, she founded the Torchwood Institute to protect Britain and its territories from aliens—with the Doctor listed as enemy number one. Bases were established in London, England (Torchwood One), Glasgow, Scotland (Torchwood Two), and Cardiff, Wales (Torchwood Three).

Window was originally a marine outlet pump

JACK HARKNESS

Torchwood Tower (London) was built to reach a spatial breach 600 feet above sea level.

Powerful and mysterious Rift Manipulator

## Yvonne Hartman

Over the years, the Torchwood Institute moved from battling aliens to exploiting their technology, its motto being: "If it is alien, it is ours." Under Yvonne Hartman, this attitude led to a battle between Daleks and Cybermen at Canary Wharf in London, and the destruction of the Torchwood Institute.

## A New Torchwood

After the Battle of Canary Wharf, Captain Jack returned Torchwood to its original ethos of defending the Earth. Torchwood Three's HQ, the "Hub," lies under the Oval Basin in Cardiff's Bute Docks. It has many levels reaching deep underground and may be entered via an invisible lift in Roald Dahl Plass, or a disused tourist information center.

## Jack in Charge

Captain Jack has been at Torchwood for over a century. He recruited a new team to run Torchwood Three: Suzie Costello, Dr. Owen Harper, Toshiko Sato, and Ianto Jones. Suzie was later replaced by police officer Gwen Cooper. Jack is fiercely loyal to his team, even to the point of turning down an opportunity to rejoin the Doctor to stay with them. He inspires loyalty in return, although his refusal to explain his elusive past can cause resentment.

## Torchwood Team

Ianto Jones and Gwen Cooper use the Rift to provide the power to tow the Earth back home after the planet is abducted by Daleks.

# UNIT

THE UNIFIED INTELLIGENCE TASKFORCE (UNIT) was set up in the late twentieth century to deal with the alien menaces facing humankind. Although its remit is similar to Torchwood's, UNIT is a predominantly military organization. The Doctor once spent several years as UNIT's scientific advisor after he was exiled to Earth by the Time Lords for meddling in the affairs of other planets.

Dark clothes to match black uniforms worn by UNIT troops

Civilian clothing with a slight military tone

Located beneath the Tower of London is UNIT's HQ, which also houses a vast store of alien artifacts known as the Black Archive. The collection is considered so dangerous that the security protocols surrounding it are the most stringent on Earth. People's minds are automatically erased each time they leave so that they forget what they saw, and in the event of an alien incursion, a nuclear warhead can be exploded to destroy its contents.

When three versions of the Doctor become imprisoned in the Tower of London in 1562, the Eleventh Doctor scrawls a numerical sequence on the wall, hoping that modern-day UNIT will find it and realize that it's the activation code for a vortex manipulator stored in the Black Archive!

## Kate Stewart

Intelligent and strong-minded, Kate Stewart is UNIT's Chief Scientific Officer and the daughter of Brigadier Lethbridge-Stewart, the Doctor's old friend and colleague. Thanks to Kate, UNIT is now led by science rather than military might, and her leadership and investigative skills are proven to be resilient under pressure.

Striped scarf reminiscent of the Fourth Doctor's

Spare pens and inhaler for asthma kept in pocket

### Osgood

With her quirky and excitable personality, Kate Stewart's scientific assistant, Osgood, is an unconventional member of UNIT. But despite her nervous nature, she bravely helps defend UNIT HQ during the Zygons' infiltration attempt.

The Doctor has always had something of an uneasy relationship with UNIT, often disapproving of its blunt, militaristic ways. He's particularly annoyed when a UNIT helicopter airlifts his TARDIS to the National Gallery to get his attention, instead of simply asking for his help!

## The *Valiant*

UNIT's flagship, *Valiant*, is an aircraft carrier with a difference—it floats in the air, not on the sea. It was designed by evil Time Lord the Master, while he was masquerading as Mr. Saxon and working for the Ministry of Defense, and he later made it his base of operations on Earth. After the Master's defeat, UNIT readopted the ship—but not before checking it thoroughly for any Time Lord tricks. Colonel Mace uses its strong engines to disperse the Sontarans' poisonous gas.

## UNIT Armory

After years of fighting alien menaces, UNIT has amassed a stock of unusual weapons, each with a very specific purpose. Silver bullets are kept in case of a werewolf attack, while anti-Dalek shells are troops' best hope of defeating Daleks. Gold-tipped bullets are reserved for Cybermen, and following recent intelligence, rad-steel coated bullets have been added to the arsenal to overcome Sontaran defenses.

### UNIT FACTS

- Martha Jones gets a job as a UNIT medical officer following the Doctor's recommendation.
- The Doctor is still officially a member of UNIT, never having resigned. However, he has never considered himself bound by the organization's rules and regulations.
- UNIT and Torchwood reluctantly share intelligence and resources, and staff are occasionally seconded between organizations.

Pulling both cords operates teleport

Central panel conceals teleport base code

## PROJECT INDIGO TELEPORT

UNIT's experimental teleport, Project Indigo, uses technology salvaged from the Sontarans. Untested, unstabilized, and with no coordinates, it is a possible death trap. But Martha uses it anyway because she is UNIT's only hope of finding the Doctor when Davros threatens the whole universe.

## OSTERHAGEN KEY

25 nuclear warheads have been placed under the Earth's crust, so that if the suffering of the human race reaches crisis point, they can be detonated by the holders of the Osterhagen Key. When Earth faces destruction from Davros, Martha is sent by UNIT to prepare the Key for detonation. Three Osterhagen stations must be online to use the Key.

UNIT is based in Geneva but has branches worldwide. The British section was initially headed up by Brigadier Lethbridge-Stewart, and he remained its leader for many years before retiring. He was later succeeded by the likes of Colonel Mace and, eventually, Kate Stewart. The US forces in New York were commanded by General Sanchez until his tragic death during a Dalek invasion.

A UNIT soldier is always battle-ready, although many never encounter an alien.

Identification badge

UNIT "wings" cap badge, adopted in the 1990s

Reinforced helmet

In especially hazardous conditions, UNIT may also mobilize specially trained, heavily armored soldiers.

Armoured gear to protect against alien attack

UNIT PRIVATE

UNIT SOLDIER

# SARAH JANE SMITH

**F**EARLESS REPORTER Sarah Jane Smith traveled with the Third and Fourth Doctors, but when the Fourth Doctor was suddenly recalled to Gallifrey, he left her behind on Earth, without even saying goodbye. When the Doctor didn't return, Sarah Jane assumed he was dead. Many years later, they are reunited and they continue to meet when danger threatens. He has turned up in both his tenth and eleventh incarnations to help her battle alien threats.

Thirty years after he left without saying goodbye, the Doctor meets Sarah Jane when they happen to be investigating strange events at a school. However, she doesn't recognize his tenth incarnation.

## Curious Companion

Sarah Jane's natural curiosity, intelligence, and compassion make her a perfect partner for the Doctor on his adventures. Even after the Doctor leaves her, Sarah Jane devotes her career to investigating occurrences that are too strange or dangerous for other journalists to explore.

## Mr. Smith

Aiding Sarah Jane in her adventures is supercomputer, Mr. Smith. He was created through a union between her laptop and a Xylok crystal, which scans for alien threats from its attic hideaway. Among other talents, Mr. Smith can link up with all the telephone exchanges in the world.

Smart suit for carrying out investigations in school

## A Courageous Captive

Sarah Jane proves her courage when she allows herself to be taken captive by the Daleks. The Daleks transport her to Davros's Command Ship in the Medusa Cascade, where the Doctor and a group of his other companions are also being held. Sarah Jane joins forces with Jack Harkness, using her warp star to create a weapon capable of destroying the ship.

After Davros's plan is thwarted, Sarah Jane helps to pilot the TARDIS and tow Earth back to its position in the solar system.

## Motherhood

Sarah Jane adopts a young boy as her son. He was created from DNA samples by an alien race called Bane, in a quest to find the archetypal human. Sarah Jane rescues the boy and names him Luke.

# K-9

**L**OYAL AND FEARLESS, boasting vast memory banks and highly sophisticated sensors, robotic dog K-9 became indispensable to the Doctor during his fourth incarnation. He traveled everywhere with the Doctor and would defend him at all costs. When the Doctor's companion Leela decided to remain on Gallifrey, K-9 stayed with her. The Doctor then built a replacement, K-9 Mk II, and a third model was sent to Sarah Jane Smith. After K-9 Mk III is blown up defeating the Krillitane, the Doctor presents Sarah Jane with K-9 Mk IV.

Thirty years after the Doctor gave him to Sarah Jane, K-9 is not in a good shape. The British climate and salted roads have taken their toll, but fortunately the Doctor is on hand to repair his old friend.

## Old Friend

A brilliant doctor named Professor Marius created the original K-9 in the year 5000, using a mobile computer and laboratory to assist him. Even K-9's most recent incarnation, Mk IV, looks similar to the original—styled after Marius's beloved pet dog.

### K-9 FACTS

- After the first K-9 helped the Doctor defeat a sentient virus, the robot's maker, Professor Marius, gave his creation to the Time Lord so he could assist him on his travels.

- According to the Doctor, K-9's design is the height of fashion in the year 5000.

**DATA-COM PROBE (EXTENDED)**

K-9's telescopic data-com probe extends and retracts from in front of his "eyes"

Data-com probe (retracted)

Sensor can analyze all known substances

Tracking sensors

Multi-wavelength optical spectrum sensor

Gravitronic brain enables K-9's artificial intelligence

Signal booster antenna

Operator's manual console

Photon blaster

Housing for fully buffered deutronic battery

Each K-9 model is equipped with a photon blaster in the snout. This weapon demonstrates Professor Marius's awareness of potential space threats.

Name tag contains tracking beacon

Removable cover to primary drives

All-terrain protective alignment buffer

K-9 MK IV

# JOHN SMITH

JOHN SMITH—THE MOST ordinary of names—has often been the Doctor's alias of choice when wanting to blend in. But, when the Tenth Doctor needs somewhere to hide from the deadly Family of Blood, he not only adopts the name, but actually becomes John Smith. The Family is able to track a Time Lord anywhere in time or space, so the TARDIS rewrites the Doctor's DNA to make him truly human.

### JOURNAL OF IMPOSSIBLE THINGS

The Doctor's real life seeps through into John Smith's dreams, which he records as fiction in what he calls his "journal of impossible things," The TARDIS, the Doctor's old companion Rose, and many monsters feature, as well as memories of the Earth's future such as World War I (1914–1918).

Arch sends electrical charges through the body to rewrite its cellular structure

## From Doctor to Teacher

The TARDIS places John Smith in Herefordshire, England in 1913 as a history teacher at Farringham School for Boys. The disguise is so complete that Smith believes that he has always been human and is the Nottingham-born son of watchmaker Sydney and nurse Verity. He is an ordinary man of narrow experiences who knows nothing of the Doctor.

Mortarboard is symbol of authority

Human body takes the appearance of the Tenth Doctor

Human senses are dull in comparison to a Time Lord's

Cane used for corporal punishment

Books provide Smith with historical informaton

Teacher disguise built on Doctor's love of knowledge

Nurse Joan Redfern, a young war widow, is the Matron of Farringham School. Joan's unassuming but caring personality appeals to shy and insecure Smith. As an ordinary man, he can see the beauty in an ordinary woman. However, falling in love is something the Doctor never allowed for in his plan. Eventually he realizes that he must sacrifice his happiness for the greater good and return to his Time Lord existence.

Cable connects to TARDIS databanks to access physiological information

## CHAMELEON ARCH

Device used to implant a new personality

Clamp stops Time Lord from ripping off connectors while in pain

Pocket watch absorbs and stores Time Lord's physical and mental essence

The TARDIS's chameleon arch can alter a Time Lord's physiology to any compatible species without affecting his outer appearance. Once transformation is complete, a Gallifreyan fob watch – a symbol of the Time Lords' mastery over time – stores the original memories, personality and biological data, which are restored the moment the watch is opened.

## Rewriting Cells

The process of transforming every cell from Time Lord to human is agonizing. Two hearts compress into one, the body temperature rises, and the respiratory bypass system vanishes. However, because the natural physiology is eager to reassert itself, the cells return to their original shapes painlessly.

Locking mechanism

## POCKET WATCH

Appearance of an ordinary pocket watch is due to perception filter

Engraving of Gallifreyan solar system

Martha is the only one who knows the truth about John Smith. The Doctor has trusted her with his life, but in the meantime, she has to endure the racism, sexism, and classism of the early 1910s, even from John Smith himself.

## Smith the Caretaker

The Doctor has used his alias as John Smith many times in order to investigate aliens on Earth without arousing human suspicion. With a Skovox Blitzer skulking in the vicinity of Coal Hill School, the Time Lord goes undercover as the school's new caretaker, intending to corner the deadly war machine.

Winding button turns wearer invisible

## INVISIBILITY WATCH

To avoid being detected by the Skovox Blitzer, the Doctor uses an invisibility watch—an ingenious device that works by reversing light waves. The Doctor is worried that if the Skovox Blitzer detects his superior intelligence, it may self-destruct and blow up planet Earth in the process.

Caretaker's coat

SKOVOX BLITZER

Scanner detects human body heat

Battle-scarred outer shell

Powerful laser weapon

Spider-like appendages allow movement across all terrains

The Skovox Blitzer is one of the deadliest killing machines ever invented. When the warring Skovox and Overite races were wiped out, their self-replicating drones carried on fighting, and somehow one such Skovox war machine fell to Earth through a time fissure.

# DALEKS

Eye-stalk is a Dalek's weakest point

Batch recognition code of individual Dalek

Dome rotates to provide 360° field of vision

Upper casing opens to expose Dalek being

Solar-energy absorbing slats

E XTERMINATE! EXTERMINATE! The battle cry of the Daleks, and the mindset it represents, has made them feared throughout the universe. Concealed inside armored life-support casings, the Daleks are ruthless conquerors, who believe in the superiority of their own race and hold all other beings in contempt, suitable only for extermination. Across time, Dalek aggression has led to interstellar wars and encouraged alliances against them. Of all the Doctor's enemies, the Daleks are the oldest and deadliest. He has defeated them time and time again, but Daleks are resilient and driven to survive at any cost.

Tactical environment scanner grid

Telescopic manipulator arm

Death ray gun

Sensor globe

## Inside a Dalek

Daleks originated as Kaleds on the planet Skaro. A thousand-year war led to environmental contamination, causing the Kaleds to mutate and degenerate into weak, tentacled creatures.

## Genetically Modified

The Kaled scientist, Davros, built armored life-support systems to support the now tentacled Kaleds. He genetically engineered them, instilling an overwhelming drive for survival and a hatred of all other species, while magnifying their intellect and stripping them of all "unnecessary" emotions. He named the perfect "killing machine" he had created... the Dalek.

Hoverpad base conceals motive power system

## Extermination Tools

A Dalek's arm is strong enough to crush a human skull, but it can also kill by extracting all brain waves.

A Dalek's death ray gun uses a ray beam to destroy every cell in a human body.

Each warrior Dalek is equipped with a manipulator arm and a ray gun. The arm can interface with computer systems or mimic hand movements with its "sucker" made of morphic material. The "death ray" is a directed energy weapon that can stun or kill.

"Sucker" can create powerful vacuum

**MANIPULATOR ARM**

Arm extends to twice its length

**DEATH RAY GUN (FRONT VIEW)**

Nitrid barrel

Amplifier tubes manipulate strength of beam to stun or kill

Acceleration chamber projects energy beam

**DEATH RAY GUN (SIDE VIEW)**

Beam initiation generator

## Dalek Point of View

The eye-stalk of the Dalek battle armor provides enhanced vision in the natural colors of Dalek sight. Inbuilt multi-spectral sensors also allow the Dalek to see in infra-red, x-ray, and ultra-violet modes. The single eye-stalk is a Dalek's weakest point as it has no back-up system.

The brilliant and psychotic Davros created the Daleks.

## Key Dalek Battles

The Daleks have waged war across time and space since their creation, but the complexities of time travel, and the Time Lords' attempts to change Dalek history, make a comprehensive timeline of their battles and invasions difficult. Here are some of their attempts at conquest:

■ Generations after their creation, Daleks were still battling their neighbors, the **Thals**, when they were first encountered by the Doctor in his first incarnation.

■ While chasing the **First Doctor** through time, a Dalek execution squad fought, and was defeated by, the robot **Mechanoids** in the 23rd century. This was the beginning of a long war between the two races.

■ The Daleks fought another long war, over many centuries, with the android **Movellans** from star system 4-X-Alpha-4, as both tried to expand their stellar empires. When that war became stalemated, the Daleks traveled through time to seek help from their ancient creator, Davros.

■ **Reviving Davros** led to factions within the Dalek hierarchy and a series of **civil wars** between different groups supporting and opposing Davros.

■ In the 22nd century, the Daleks twice invaded **Earth**, the first time after the destruction of **World War III** and later, around Earth year **2164**, intending to turn it into a giant battleship to aid their wars of conquest.

■ By the year **4000**, the Daleks planned a master strike to **conquer the galaxy** with the aid of similarly power-hungry allies. When the Doctor defeated their plans, the alliance self-destructed and embroiled the Daleks in new conflicts.

■ Learning of the **Time Lords'** attempts to thwart their creation, the Daleks attacked Gallifrey and the **last Great Time War** began.

■ **Gallifrey** was seemingly destroyed in the attempt to wipe out the Daleks, but the **Cult of Skaro** and the **Emperor** survived. By the year 200,100, the Emperor had rebuilt the Dalek race, then largely destroyed by **Rose Tyler**.

The Daleks' casing is made from Dalekanium—an extremely robust bonded polycarbide material. It can be penetrated by bastic-tipped bullets, so the Daleks created an energy shield for additional protection.

Dalek battle armor is designed to open up, so that repairs, system enhancements, and medical treatments can be carried out. Even without its weaponry, the Dalek is a dangerous creature and has been known to kill.

To avoid capture or to atone for failing a mission, a Dalek is fitted with a self-destruct system for complete obliteration. The components of this system are mounted in the Dalek's sensor globes.

Equipped with anti-gravity generators and gyroscopic stabilization systems, Daleks can glide across any terrain or hover over any obstacle—even a steep staircase is no hindrance.

# DALEK FLAGSHIP

EMERGING FROM HIDING above Earth, the Dalek fleet is armed, dangerous, and all-powerfully gigantic. The massive flagship that commands the fleet transports the Dalek Emperor, who is worshipped as a god by the rest of the Daleks. The Emperor is wired into the ship's systems—allowing him total control. From there he can operate the entire fleet using his mind alone.

## Hidden Army

Long ago, this ship escaped from the Great Time War, slipping away into "the dark space." It had one lone, badly injured Dalek onboard, who became the Emperor. Over the centuries, the Emperor hatched a plan to harvest humans from Earth to supply the genetic material for a host of new Daleks. For this end, the flagship is teeming with a Dalek army, poised to attack Earth.

### FLAGSHIP FACTS

- The flagship was used during the Great Time War between Daleks and Time Lords.
- The Dalek Emperor intends to create "Heaven on Earth" by bombing the planet until it is radioactive rubble.
- Rose destroys the Dalek fleet, including the flagship, when she gains enormous powers from looking into the time-space vortex at the heart of the TARDIS.

DALEK EMPEROR'S LIFE-TANK

Hull strengthening plate

Armor-plating in spaceship-grade Dalekanium (bonded polycarbide metal)

Signal transmitter ring

Heavy polycarbide rivets

Ship energy-shielding pulses

Rotating dome and outer ring create spin that propels ship

Giant hangar openings located around the central disc allow millions of Daleks to emerge at once into the void of space, heading toward Earth.

Power/communication spikes

Dalek Emperor at center of control room

Hull damage from the Great Time War

Supercomputer housing connected to all systems aboard the ship

TARDIS

Acceleration compensator

Armored shielding

Computer power feed assembly

Storage vats for molten polycarbide used in Dalek manufacture

Housing for humans awaiting "processing"

Science labs where Daleks extract from human captives the one cell in a billion considered fit to be nurtured into a Dalek

The Dalek Emperor masterminds operations from a fortified chamber at the center of the ship. A breathable atmosphere in the room allows human captives to be brought before him for inspection. Their fate is sealed when the Emperor selects one of two grappling hooks situated below his life-tank, deciding whether or not they are eligible for DNA harvesting.

Shield generator array

Computer core

Reactor/power generator

Computer systems matrix

Ventilation/cooling vanes

Dalek training hangar

Vertical transport shaft

Overseer observation platforms

Torpedo ports arrayed around central axis

Hangar doors

Daleks arranged in formation, ready for battle

Cell array around which electromagnetic pulses travel to create rotation for forward movement

Dalek manufacturing hangars

# DAVROS

**D** AVROS IS RESPONSIBLE for creating the Daleks. The scientist foresaw a day when the chemical warfare that raged on his home planet would cause his people, the Kaleds, to mutate. Obsessed with the survival of his race, he experimented with their mutations and invented an armored machine to carry them. Ambitious Davros then went further, making chromosomal changes to Dalek embryos to remove their consciences and emotions. But his plan backfired when his creations declared him unnecessary to their plans and attempted to kill him.

Davros enjoys taunting the Tenth Doctor. He claims that the Doctor is responsible for innocent deaths, despite his abhorrence of violence, as he takes ordinary people and turns them into weapons to die in his name.

Like many children with their parents, the Daleks' relationship with Davros is a combination of reverence and contempt. They look to him to solve their problems, but still believe that they are better off without him.

## Insane Leader

The Doctor regards Davros as one of the most dangerous, and certainly the most insane, of his enemies. While the Time Lord has a grudging respect for some of his adversaries, Davros is not one of them. The Doctor is unsurprised to discover that the events of the Time War have inspired bitter Davros to want to destroy all living things.

Microphone and amplifier enable speech

Single lens replaces sightless eyes

Face scarred by his accident

Heart and lung machine keeps Davros alive

Mechanical fingertips shoot energy bolts

Wheelchair generates its own power

Every Dalek creature has been grown from a cell taken from Davros's body. The Daleks' proud creator revels in the idea that all his "children" are literally his own flesh and blood.

## Davros's Accident

Davros's pride will not let him speak of the accident that maimed him. Yet a lesser creature would have died from the injuries that left him with only a head, torso, and one withered arm and hand (later shot off and replaced with a mechanical copy). A single blue lens gives him sight since his eyes are withered. His hearing and voice are also artificially aided. Davros's technical genius has prolonged his life far beyond its natural span.

Frictionless base allows silent movement

Controls life-support functions

Motor and directional controls

Daleks remote control

Remote control to regulate the environment

Chair inspired the design of the Dalek shell

Chair can adopt hover mode

Signal to summon Daleks

Operates suspended-animation field

Connection point for external electrical devices

### WEELCHAIR CONTROL PANEL

Davros's customized wheelchair helps him get around—and it also keeps him alive. Without the chair's life-support system, Davros would not survive for even 30 seconds. Davros has turned this weakness into a tool, building devices into the chair that can help him further his evil plans of total destruction.

# THE GENESIS ARK

**W**HEN THE SECRETIVE Torchwood Institute attempts to harness energy from a spatial disturbance over London, it unwittingly breaks through a wall between dimensions. A sinister metal sphere emerges through the breach, which the Doctor instantly recognizes as a Void Ship—containing the Genesis Ark. Sensing that nothing good can be inside it, the Doctor urges Torchwood to send it back through the Rift.

## THE VOID SHIP

This hypothetical craft was designed to exist outside space and time, traveling between dimensions. The sphere fills all who go near it with foreboding. In theory it does not exist because it lacks both radiation and atomic mass.

When the Void Ship activates, Torchwood's lab screens go wild with readings that show that the object suddenly has height, mass, and an electromagnetic field. The Sphere Chamber doors immediately seal shut to put the area in automatic quarantine.

## Dalek Transporter

A sinister casket is concealed inside the Void Ship. Known as the Genesis Ark, it has dimensionally transcendental Time Lord technology similar to the TARDIS, and was used during the Great Time War for the sole purpose of imprisoning the armies of the Time Lords' deadliest enemy—the Daleks.

### The Ark's Purpose

As the Ark is activated in the sky above London, the Doctor finally understands what the Daleks meant by "Time Lord science." Like the TARDIS, the Ark is much larger on the inside than on the outside. It was used as a prison ship for the millions of the Daleks captured during the Great Time War.

Dalek Sec elevates the Ark the 48 square kilometers needed for activation.

Casing designed to prime mechanisms when touched by handprint radiation

Encryption mechanism

Impenetrable hull

Vectral frame clamp

Life support monitor

Red light indicates priming console has been activated

Sensor processing unit

Elevation engine

Radioactive steam vent

## The Key to the Ark

Rose and Mickey witness the Genesis Ark and four Daleks—the Cult of Skaro—emerging from the Void Ship. The Daleks must keep Rose and Mickey alive because a time-traveler's touch is the key that opens the Ark. As humanoid time-travelers, Rose and Mickey soak up the universe's background radiation—the power source for the Ark. When fighting rages between Daleks and Cybermen in the sphere chamber, Mickey is shoved against the Ark and touches it, causing it to activate.

When the Void Ship bursts through the breach in time and space, it is followed by a small army of humanoid, ghostly figures. The "ghosts" are soon revealed to be Cybermen, entering from a parallel world, intent on invading.

## The Battle of Canary Wharf, London

As soon as the Void Ship opens, Daleks and Cybermen detect each other's presence. A historic exchange begins as the two rival races, who have never encountered each other before, refuse to identify themselves to the other. Talking leads to fighting: airborne Dalek legions from the Genesis Ark begin a spectacular battle with the parallel-world Cybermen. Leader Dalek Sec orders his airborne forces to exterminate all life forms below in Canary Wharf, but the Dalek supremacy is short-lived. The Doctor opens the breach once more, sucking almost every Dalek and Cyberman back into the Void.

### CYBER EAR-PIECE

The Cybermen use cyber ear-pieces to control some of the members of Torchwood. The only way for the link to be destroyed is to disrupt the signal—which proves fatal to the wearers of the ear-pieces.

Neck strap

Transporter disc

Charged metal alloy

The Parallel World Transporter is worn around the neck and can transport only one person at a time safely. It is used by a group of humans from a parallel Earth, who materialize into Torchwood to help in the fight against the emerging Cybermen.

### PARALLEL WORLD TRANSPORTER

The Ark releases millions of Daleks over London. The Battle Daleks organize themselves into flying squadrons of 12 or 16.

# DALEK SEC

A S LEADER OF THE Cult of Skaro, Dalek Sec is tasked by the Dalek Emperor with finding new ways for Daleks to breed and prosper. Following a failed plan to grow Dalek embryos, the ambitious Sec comes up with a radical idea: purity has led to near extinction for the Daleks, so he decides their biological destiny lies with humans, in what he calls the Final Experiment.

## Fanatical Leader

The utterly ruthless Dalek Sec is the Black Dalek leader of the Cult of Skaro, guiding the research of his colleagues. These select Daleks have a strong bond of loyalty to each other, and are driven by the need to extend the Dalek Empire throughout space and time. Under the leadership of Sec, the Cult dedicates its existence to finding new ways to exterminate the Daleks' adversaries, by creatively thinking in "non-Dalek" ways. Like their leader, each Dalek is assigned its own name and personality, in the belief that understanding and mimicking the individuality of many of their enemies will allow them to discover new and more terrifying ways to overcome them.

Dalek is equipped with automatic distress call if casing is breached

Swiveling eye-stalk and rotating dome provide almost spherical field of vision

Forcefield broadcast antennae

Rotating mid-section gives Dalek 360° range of fire

Death ray beam emitter sends out an immense electrical discharge

Sensor globes capable of free flight provide remote battlefield intelligence

Luminosity discharge valve dissipates excess energy from Dalek's cells, through light and sound emission

Sensor grid louvers allow waste heat exhaust

Manipulator arm's telescopic tube and swivel mount provide tremendous reach

"Sucker" tool, made of morphic material, can assume various useful shapes

Dalekanium outer casing is lightweight, yet incredibly strong

Hoverpad base with anti-gravity generators enables Dalek to hover and fly

The Cult members escaped the destruction of the Dalek race at the end of the Great Time War by fleeing in a Void Ship with the captured Genesis Ark. Their ship used a spatial disturbance to break through to Earth.

## CULT OF SKARO FACTS

◼ The Cult of Skaro consists of four members, led by Dalek Sec. This small number can be strategically useful, but they are too few to be a military threat on their own.

◼ The Cult is named after the Dalek homeworld Skaro, which was devastated by a supernova generated by the Seventh Doctor. The planet was finally obliterated during the Great Time War.

◼ In order to "think like the enemy," the Cult Daleks are encouraged to develop their imaginations.

◼ Unlike ordinary Daleks, Cult members do have some emotions, which mimic those of other life forms. They also have a sense of self-preservation that is not found in Dalek warriors.

◼ The Cult's existence was kept so secret by the Daleks that even the Doctor thought they were a legend.

DALEK CAAN

DALEK JAST

DALEK THAY

All four members of the Cult of Skaro—Sec, Thay, Jast, and Caan, were present when the Genesis Ark, a ship containing millions of Daleks, was sent back into the Void—a rift in time and space between parallel worlds—by the Doctor. To escape this failure, Sec transports the four members of the Cult away, using an emergency temporal shift.

# CULT OF SKARO

A SECRET ORDER OF Daleks, the Cult of Skaro, consists of four members. Their role is to think like the enemies of the Daleks in order to find new ways of exterminating them. They exist outside the normal Dalek hierarchy, above even the chief Dalek, the Emperor. To emphasize their special status, they even have individual names—Sec, Thay, Jast, and Caan.

In 1930, New York City is in the grip of an economic depression, with mass unemployment and thousands destitute. The Doctor and his companion Martha turn up here soon after the Daleks arrive.

## Becoming Human

Dalek Sec is so dedicated that he is willing to experiment upon himself. He becomes the first ever Dalek-human hybrid. The other three members of the Cult of Skaro—Daleks Thay, Jast, and Caan—believe that Daleks should remain pure, but Sec disagrees. He is convinced that a genetic merger with humans will herald the beginning of a new era of Dalek rule.

Dalek mutant merges with human brains

Chromatin solution stimulates genetic changes

Casing and weapons are discarded after metamorphosis

Dalekanium casing acts as chrysalis during transformation

DALEK INTERIOR

## Energy Converter

Dalek Sec's plan to forge a new Dalek-human race requires a powerful energy source. A huge solar flare is due to pass by Earth, and will provide the necessary Gamma radiation. The Daleks must attract the flare and conduct its energy, so they engineer and build the tallest point in New York—the Empire State Building.

Mind wiped of human memories

### PIG SLAVES

Intelligence determines the fate of the humans captured by the Daleks. While those of superior intelligence are kept for the Final Experiment, less clever prisoners are transformed into primitive pig slaves and used to abduct more people. The pig genes are chosen for their relative hardiness.

## Dalek-Human Hybrid

Ambition, hatred, aggression, and a genius for war—that is what Dalek Sec thinks being human is all about. When he combines with the ruthless and ambitious Mr. Diagoras, he believes he is getting more of the same. But Sec discovers something unexpected—positive emotions. He decides that Daleks must return to emotions—both positive and negative ones.

Human brain creates emotions

Tentacles from Dalek mutant

Exposed flesh makes hybrid vulnerable

Mr Diagoras's suit is a remnant of a former identity

Hybrid gains dextrous fingers

DALEK SEC—
MR. DIAGORAS
HYBRID

## Dalek Humans

Human DNA is spliced with Dalek Sec's genetic code, creating a new race. But some Time Lord gets in the mix, and the humanoid Daleks turn from unblinking servitude and begin to question orders. This leads to their extermination, but not before they kill Daleks Thay and Jast.

### Dalek Caan

With Daleks Sec, Thay, and Jast all dead, Dalek Caan is the only surviving member of the Cult of Skaro—the last Dalek in the universe. Caan rejects the Doctor's offer of help, operates his emergency temporal shift, and vanishes.

## Hooverville

Solomon, the leader of New York shanty town Hooverville, cares for his fellow outcasts, but when he tries to extend the hand of friendship to the Daleks, he is exterminated. However, his courage inspires Dalek Sec, who feels compassion for the first time.

The purpose of Daleks is to be supreme! Sec's fellow Daleks disagree that their race should renounce their purpose by embracing emotions and becoming humanized. They declare their one-time leader to be an enemy of the Daleks, and he is exterminated while compassionately trying to save the Doctor's life.

# DAVROS'S EMPIRE

MEGALOMANIAC EMPEROR DAVROS has only one ambition—to see a universe ruled by Daleks. Rescued from the Time War, his warped mind believes that co-operation between species is impossible and that ultimately only one race can survive; he is determined that race will be the Daleks. His plans are based on the Daleks annihilating every other being in the universe. This apocalyptic short-cut will make Davros Emperor of an empty infinity.

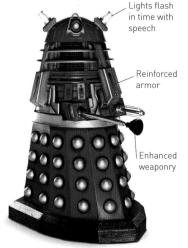

Lights flash in time with speech

Reinforced armor

Enhanced weaponry

## The Supreme Dalek

Although Daleks were engineered to have no emotions, the Supreme Dalek is guilty of pride when it believes that the Daleks have finally triumphed over the Doctor. Charged with activating the Reality Bomb, its strength and determination see it retain control as other Daleks falter, but it meets its end thanks to Captain Jack Harkness.

Arm raised in glee at destruction

DAVROS

## Bomb Maker

In order to build his empire and destroy all life forms other than the Daleks, crazed Davros creates the Reality Bomb. This fearsome technology cancels out the electrical fields that hold together atoms, obliterating the fabric of reality itself. Davros wants to see the Daleks exterminate their way to victory.

## Dalek Caan

The only surviving member of the Cult of Skaro, Dalek Caan went insane when he jumped into the Time War to save Davros. This mind-altering experience brought him the gift of prophecy.

The Dalek Command Ship, the *Crucible*, has a core of deadly z-neutrino energy.

## The Medusa Cascade

27 celestial bodies, including Earth, Adipose 3, Pyrovillia, Callufrax Minor, Jahoo, Shallacatop, Woman Wept, Clom, and the Lost Moon of Poosh, vanish from their normal orbits and appear together in the Medusa Cascade. This is not chance, but careful design by Davros. In their new formation, with the Dalek *Crucible* at their center, they function as a transmitter designed to focus the wavelength of the Reality Bomb.

## Masters of Earth

Once again, Daleks terrorize the citizens of Earth. This time, however, they set their sights higher than the destruction of the human race: Earth has a role to play as part of the machinery of the Reality Bomb.

## The Subwave Network

The Subwave Network is a piece of undetectable sentient software used to seek out and communicate with anyone who can help to contact the Doctor. Sarah Jane Smith uses her computer, Mr. Smith, to connect them all from different places in time and space.

Ex-Prime Minister Harriet Jones feels responsible for Earth's citizens, and sacrifices her life to help contact the Doctor.

## The Secret Army

The Subwave Network enables the Doctor to communicate with Captain Jack Harkness, Sarah Jane Smith, and Martha Jones— previous companions of the Doctor, collectively called "the Children of Time" by Davros. Together, they help the Doctor fight the Daleks.

The Mr. Copper Foundation developed the Subwave Network used by Harriet Jones.

## The Shadow Proclamation

Nearly all species recognize the authority of the Shadow Proclamation, an imposing galactic regulatory body and police force that both sets and enforces laws. Its directives proscribe alien interference with planets and their populations, and govern the rules of parlay between species.

Distinctive albino appearance

### THE ARCHITECT

An elegant, pale humanoid figure, known as the Architect, speaks on behalf of the Shadow Proclamation.

The Judoon are hired as enforcers and bodyguards for doing the Shadow Proclamation's work. The muscle-bound creatures are perfect for situations that require a show of force.

## SHADOW PROCLAMATION FACTS

- Protocol allows representatives to seize transport and technology.
- The Shadow Proclamation has its own religious creed that includes a sole god.

HEADQUARTERS OF THE SHADOW PROCLAMATION

## The End of the Daleks

The Doctor is reluctant to take a life, but his half-human, half-Time Lord incarnation has no qualms about destroying the whole Dalek race. This version of the Doctor blasts the Dalekanium power feeds, annihilating the Daleks and their ship, and bringing an end to Davros and his evil plans.

# DALEK ASYLUM

**I**MPRISONED ON A SNOW-CAPPED PLANET deep in space are the most dangerously insane Daleks the universe has never seen—feared even by their own kind. This asylum planet is protected by a forcefield, somehow damaged when a spaceship crash-lands there. Fearing that the abandoned, unhinged Daleks will escape and wreak havoc on their jailers, the Daleks' governing body—the Parliament—resorts to desperate measures and turns to the Doctor for help.

The Parliament ship is equipped with a gravity beam, which is powerful enough to penetrate the asylum planet's forcefield. The Doctor, Amy, and Rory are catapulted by it toward the planet at incredible speed. The beam also cushions their landing to prevent serious injury.

The Dalek Parliament is a huge spaceship protected by a fleet of saucers. Inside the heavily armed vessel are countless ranks of bronze Daleks who are presided over by the Dalek Prime Minister. When they're first brought aboard the ship, the Doctor and his friends are kept in a holding cell directly below the vast hall.

Battle-damaged outer shell

## Deranged Daleks

The asylum extends to the core of the planet and is filled with millions of battle-scarred Daleks, surviving in a dormant state. One particular area—the Dalek equivalent of "intensive care"—contains the crazed survivors of wars on planets such as Spiridon, Kembel, Aridius, Vulcan, and Exxilon. In other words, these are the Daleks that survived an encounter with the Doctor himself, and so, are unlikely to look kindly on him.

Unlike its inferiors, the Dalek Prime Minister is housed in a glass casing which allows the Kaled mutant within to be fully visible.

Dalek inside rests in a dormant state

Casing covered in dirt and rust from asylum

### OSWIN OSWALD

A young junior entertainment officer named Oswin Oswald is apparently the sole survivor of the spaceship *Alaska* after it crashes into the asylum world. She intrigues the Doctor with her ability to hack into the Dalek's advanced systems. The truth is that Oswin has been fully converted into a Dalek within the asylum, but subconsciously chose to deny it.

Belt full of high-tech gadgets

In order to capture the Doctor and his friends, the Dalek Parliament uses humanoid slaves who have been conditioned to serve their masters without question. When one of these puppets is activated, a Dalek eyestalk extends from its head, while a powerful gunstick protrudes from the palm of its hand.

Primitive Dalek casing

# IRONSIDES

IN WORLD WAR II, the constant bombing of the Blitz pushes Britain to the brink of despair. But Professor Bracewell offers hope: he has invented robots with greater firepower than any other human-made weapon—the Ironsides. Destructive but obedient, they appear to be both the perfect soldier and the perfect servant. However, the Ironsides are truly Daleks plotting an elaborate scheme to ensnare the Doctor.

Positronic brain

## PROFESSOR EDWIN BRACEWELL

Scottish scientist Professor Bracewell is extremely proud of his fearsome and loyal Ironsides, whom he believes will stop the war. He is stunned to discover that he didn't make them, and, in fact, they made him. He is simply an android, implanted with false memories of another human's life. The Daleks were using him as part of their plan.

Bracewell is powered by an Oblivion Continuum—a captured wormhole, that, if detonated, would destroy the Earth.

Union flag shows apparent allegiance to Great Britain

Ironsides have kit bags, just like soldiers

Suction cup for fetching files and carrying tea trays

Painted khaki, like soldiers' fatigues

## The Perfect Warrior

Everyone except the Doctor thinks that the Ironsides are subservient robots, invented by Professor Bracewell. The deadly fighting machines offer assistance in any way they can to fool the humans— even serving cups of tea—and their deadly firepower is capable of blowing enemy aircraft out of the sky.

Famous "V" for Victory sign

1940s tailoring

## Winston Churchill

Although suspicious at first that the Ironsides are too good to be true, Prime Minister Winston Churchill quickly sees the potential of these killing machines, and is eager to harness their power. He uses the Ironsides to exterminate Nazi aircraft, and refuses to listen to the Doctor. Churchill cannot see a downside to Bracewell's obedient robots.

The subservience of the Ironsides doesn't fool the Doctor for a moment. In frustration, he attacks one of them, and repeats his name and their true identity. Finally, the Ironsides reveal the truth: they are Daleks and they have been waiting for this testimony from the Doctor to unleash the next part of their plan.

# PARADIGM DALEKS

**M**ILLENNIA AGO, the Daleks seeded the universe with Progenitors, devices carrying Davros's pure Dalek DNA. Their creators lost track of them and the Progenitors became a legend. But in a crippled ship, three Daleks lived on with one of these mythical devices. When the Doctor is tricked into activating it, the resurrection of a shiny new breed of so-called Paradigm Daleks begins.

## Restoration of the Daleks

Larger and more powerful than previous Daleks, the new super race of Daleks plans to breed a new army—vaster, deadlier and more cunning than ever. The first five to emerge represent familiar Dalek ranks, but redesigned: the white Supreme Dalek leader, the orange Scientist, the blue battle-planning Strategist, the yellow Eternal, and the red fighter Drone.

### THE PROGENITOR

Impenetrable casing

Designed to store pure Dalek DNA, the Progenitor is the key to rebuilding the Dalek race and can be operated only by Daleks. Because the Progenitor does not recognize the impure Daleks, they cannot activate it. Instead, they concoct a plan to use the Doctor's testimony that they are Daleks to unlock the machine and begin the resurrection process.

### MAIN CENTRAL CONTROL PANEL

The buttons on the control panel of the Dalek ship carrying the Progenitors are shaped to be operated by Dalek sucker tools.

Larger, reinforced Dalekanium casing houses superior organic creature

Sucker tool is ideally suited to Dalek machinery, but can morph for other needs

## A New Race

In order to survive over the millennia, the three Daleks protecting the Progenitors have become contaminated with other DNA and are no longer recognized as pure Dalek. Once they have engineered the new, clean race of Paradigm Daleks, they willingly submit to their extermination—nothing impure is tolerated by this terrible race.

THE SUPREME

THE SCIENTIST

Unlike the eye-stalk of the impure Daleks, behind the eye-stalk of the new true breed is a living, blood-shot organic eye.

## Stone Progenitor Dalek

The Paradigm Daleks failed in their attempt to destroy Earth. However, some, including the Supreme, escaped and returned to help trap the Doctor in the Pandorica when all believed the Time Lord was responsible for bringing about the end of time. All-consuming energy leaking through the crack in time and space leaves a stone imprint residue of the Dalek as it ceases to exist. When the Doctor successfully resets the universe, these Daleks are erased from all history, past, and present.

A blast of Alpha Mezon through the eye-stalk is fatal

Weapons still functional as dormant stone Dalek can come alive again

THE STRATEGIST

Improved scanner

Bonded polycarbide in Dalekanium now in bright colors

Red color of Drone commander

THE ETERNAL

THE DRONE

Broken lights lead soldiers to believe Dalek is deactivated and therefore safe to disassemble

Supplementary cortex vault brain keeps Dalek pure and full of hatred

Weapons non functional due to fractured fuel cell

Low, cramped tunnel in eyestalk allows access for miniaturized Doctor, Clara, and soldiers

Damage caused by explosion

# INSIDE A DALEK

ONBOARD THE SPACESHIP *Aristotle* in the Ryzak solar system, a damaged Dalek has been taken prisoner after it was found floating and abandoned in space. The mutant inside has been badly injured—to the extent that it has apparently turned good—and the Doctor agrees to be miniaturized so he can enter the Dalek's casing and give it the urgent medical attention it needs. But while a face-to-face encounter with a Dalek is perilous enough, being inside one is even more dangerous.

## Damaged Dalek

Nicknamed Rusty by the Doctor, the injured Dalek has been poisoned by leaking radiation from one of its damaged power cells. The radiation has had the extraordinary effect of expanding the mutant's consciousness, causing it to develop a new sense of morality. However, after the Doctor repairs the damage, he's horrified to discover that the Dalek immediately reverts back to its normal, murderous self, exterminating any perceived enemy in its way—including the soldiers onboard the *Aristotle*.

## RUSTY – FRONT VIEW

## RUSTY – BACK VIEW

Wires put in place to monitor any activity

## COLONEL MORGAN BLUE

As brave and fiercely determined as his niece, Colonel Morgan Blue is the man in charge of the spaceship *Aristotle* and its Dalek prisoner. When the Dalek goes on its killing spree, the Colonel makes a hard decision and commands Journey to destroy the creature at all costs—even if it means sacrificing his beloved niece in the process.

Insignia of the *Aristotle* spaceship

Flecks of white in beard from many years spent fighting Daleks

Powerful sidearm does not inspire the Doctor's trust

## LIEUTENANT JOURNEY BLUE

A member of the Combined Galactic Resistance, Journey Blue is a tough young soldier who leads the mission to enter the Dalek' casing. Her orders are to help heal the creature's injuries, but when it suddenly starts exterminating every human in sight, Journey changes the objective of the mission, and instead, decides to try to destroy the Dalek from within.

Comms unit functions even when miniaturized

Nano-controller can either maintain or reverse the state of compression

Grenades

Heavy-duty combat clothing

## The Doctor and the Dalek

The Doctor plugs his own mind into the mutant's in a bid to show it the wonder of creation, but the creature instead becomes fascinated by the Doctor's hatred of its species and transforms into a Dalek-killer. The Doctor is left troubled by the fact that there is good in the Daleks—but is there any in himself?

# CYBERMEN

THE FEARSOME CYBERNETIC CYBERMEN have cropped up at different points across space and time. Practically immortal, immensely strong and without emotion, they form a vast silver army that marches relentlessly on, chanting, "Delete, delete, delete!" On a parallel Earth, Cybermen are created by bonding human brains within a strong steel shell. Their inventor, John Lumic, believes they are the next stage of human evolution.

## Men of Steel

Cybermen may retain their human brains, but any human feelings are suppressed with an emotional inhibitor. They have an artificially grown nervous system that enables the brain to control their metal bodies and electronic parts. The steel armor is made up of a super-strong exterior shell (an exoskeleton) and a more flexible interior casing.

BACK VIEW

Many of the first humans converted into Cybermen are stored in rows in the underground cooling tunnels that fan out from the Cyber factory. These Cybermen have been placed in suspended animation by lowering the temperature inside their cybernetic armor to just above freezing point.

Visual receptors

Exoskeleton increases upper body strength

Voicebox

Cybus Industries logo conceals an emotional inhibitor

Fingertips have touch-sensitive pads

Electrodes on hands deliver fatal electric shocks

Super-strong armor protects the forearms

Chestplate shields the thermionic generator

Articulated armor for flexibility around lower torso

Coolant lines maintain low temperature inside the armor

Hip joint links exoskeleton to core armor

## CYBERMEN FACTS

- A Cyberman's armor is made from an extremely strong manganese-steel alloy.

- All Cybermen's brains are linked to form a single collective consciousness.

- The human brain inside the Cyber-armor is stored at 42.8 degrees Fahrenheit in a patented solution.

- Each individual Cyberman is powered by a thermionic generator.

## Weaponry

John Lumic's company, Cybus Industries, has a weapons division that dominates the global arms market. The Cybermen's energy weapons are created in Lumic's Blue Skies laboratory, which specializes in experimental technology. This particle beam gun is capable of delivering a pulse that is deadly to humans.

Each Cyberman's particle beam gun is powered by hydrogen gas and fires beams of deadly electrons. It has an outsized grip to fit a Cyberman's large hands but can also be fitted onto the body at the arm.

Kevlar-lined coolant lines are resistant to gunfire

Exposed coolant lines are vulnerable to attack

Leg armor extends upwards to protect knee joint

Articulated foot armor

Exoskeleton provides extra strength at thigh

Armor around calf is designed to flex during movement

Ankle joint, a point of weakness

FRONT VIEW

# CYBUS INDUSTRIES

A MASSIVE BUSINESS empire called Cybus Industries controls the global media, finance, communications, property, and technology on a parallel Earth. When the TARDIS crashes on this planet, the Doctor and his companions are curious about the huge organization. Its mega-rich but dying leader, John Lumic, has secretly spent years and millions of dollars researching human immortality. His plan is to "upgrade" humanity into a race of immortal Cybermen.

## John Lumic

The founder of Cybus Industries is a scientific genius whose inventions have made him the most powerful man on Earth. But he suffers from a terrible wasting disease that has confined him to a wheelchair and will ultimately kill him. Power and the fear of death have turned him into an insane megalomaniac who sees mortality as the ultimate enemy. To him, humanity and individuality are expendable in his narrow-minded search for an end to death.

## Air Ship

With crime rampant on the streets of parallel Britain and a night-time curfew in place, Britain's wealthy elite has taken to living in giant air ships floating above London. These zeppelins are manufactured by Cybus Industries, whose leader, John Lumic, has his own luxury model. His ship has a transmitter from which he can send instructions and signals to people's EarPods.

Bow is reinforced to withstand headwinds

EarPod transmitter

Satellite transmitter

Doses of medication delivered intravenously

Oxygen tank

Breathing apparatus

Motion control lever

Cybus Industries logo

LUMIC'S CHAIR

Rigid hull, made from a light aluminium alloy

Spotlights, used when landing airship in darkness

Horizontal fin for stability

Bridge at front of gondola

Gondola with accommodation and facilities for passengers and crew

Starboard propeller

Ventral fin

Port propeller for forward thrust

On this parallel Earth, everyone wears an EarPod. Developed by Cybus Industries, these sophisticated communications devices download news and entertainment directly into the user's brain and exert a form of mind control.

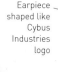

Earpiece shaped like Cybus Industries logo

Microwave antenna

Durable plastic polymer coating

EARPOD

## The Cybus Factory

Lumic secretly converts the disused buildings at Battersea Power Station in London into a factory for creating Cybermen. This is just one of many similar factories around the world. As Lumic attempts to perfect his cyber-conversion techniques, many of London's homeless people are abducted and experimented on. Inside the factory, there are hundreds of cylindrical conversion chambers. Each chamber is designed to transform a human into a Cyberman in less than a minute. The factory is capable of converting thousands of people a day into emotionless Cybermen.

The brain is the only part of a human that survives inside a Cyberman. Lumic has to find a way to remove the human brain without killing it. He realizes that speed is vital. With pain receptors in the brain deactivated by EarPods, the powerful cutting gear cuts open the human skull, carves out the brain, and transfers it into its new metal home in seconds. The remaining body is simply incinerated.

A Cyberman's human brain is housed in its steel helmet. Once in place, the brain is flooded with a chilled protein solution that preserves and nurtures it, eliminating cellular decay.

Bundle of fiberoptic cable carries data

Tubes inject coolant into Cyber Controller's body

Transparent brain-case

Throne constructed from titanium alloy

Steel body armor

## The Cyber Controller

Cybermen-creator, John Lumic, is transformed into the Cyber Controller, the leader of the Cybermen. Unlike the rest of the Cybermen, the Cyber Controller retains the emotions of anger and hatred, and his voicebox mimics Lumic's actual voice. The Cyber Controller is physically connected to a Cyber Throne. From there, he is able to control the activity of all the Cybermen.

An emotional inhibitor removes a Cyberman's human feelings. When it is deactivated, the Cybermen are killed by the mental trauma.

# THE CYBERKING

W**HEN THE CYBERMEN** were sucked into the Void during the Battle of Canary Wharf, the Doctor thought he had seen the end of them. But a few survived and broke back into the world, using a time-traveling Dimension Vault stolen from the Daleks. They arrived in London in December 1851 and set about creating the CyberKing—a giant battleship to lead their invasion of Earth and the conversion of the human population into Cybermen.

Command center

Internal Cyber-conversion unit

Mortar launcher

Laser blaster

Human brain visible inside Cybercasing

Distinctive black visor

Wide, heavy metal feet can crush people and destroy buildings

Severe hairstyle

Mercy Hartigan, Matron of the St Joseph's workhouse, deeply resents the men who oppress womankind. She accepts the Cybermen's offer of liberation, not realizing that they plan to incorporate her into the CyberKing. But strong-minded Mercy retains her emotions after conversion and bends the Cybermen to her will, combining their logic and strength with her fury and passion.

Scarlet dress chosen to cause outrage to Victorian society

### MISS MERCY HARTIGAN

## Robotic Battleship

The CyberKing is a vast, dreadnought-class battleship, 200 feet tall and fashioned in the rough shape of a Cyberman. Lumbering through London, it dwarfs any structure on Earth and wreaks devastation with mammoth-sized weapons in its arms.

## CYBERKING FACTS

▪ **Inside the CyberKing's chest is a Cyber-conversion unit, capable of transforming millions of humans and other organic life forms into Cybermen.**

▪ **The CyberKing runs on electricity. In order to generate electricity in Victorian London, the Cybermen use coal, which is shoveled by armies of kidnapped workhouse children.**

▪ **Creating Cybershades requires less power than full Cybermen, allowing the Cyberleader to concentrate resources on preparing the CyberKing.**

## The Cyberleader

Taking direct control of Cyberforces is the Cyberleader. He is easily distinguished from his all-silver troops by the black details on his helmet. If his body is destroyed then his knowledge and functions are downloaded into another Cyberman, who is then upgraded. If this is not immediately possible, the Cyberleader's program is beamed back to a control computer and stored.

Four-legged walking stance

CYBERSHADE

Metal "ears" transmit audio data

Mouth can hiss but not form words

Flexible fingers

Cybershades are created by placing the brain of a small creature, such as a cat or dog, inside a cybernetic form instead of the usual human. These cyborgs have less intelligence than their Cybermen masters, but possess more speed and agility, can outrun humans, and can scale vertical surfaces. The obedient creatures act as the Cybermen's eyes and ears in London, providing visual and audio data.

# HEDGEWICK'S WORLD

ONCE THE BIGGEST amusement park in the universe, Hedgewick's World has become an abandoned ruin. However, an army of Cybermen are entombed there, awaiting the arrival of a suitable life form to convert into a new Cyber-Planner. When the Doctor visits the planet, the cyborgs believe he will help make the next version of the Cybermen completely unbeatable.

Head swivels 360°

Blaster built into arm

Hand can detach to mount its own attack

## The Cyberiad

This new breed of Cybermen is controlled by a Cyberiad: a collective consciousness that allows their Cyber-Planners to control any individual Cyberman. This hive mind also enables all of the Cybermen to pool their processing power to solve a problem, and can distribute software patches to upgrade individual cyber units—to be resistant to electrocution, for example.

Cybernetic parts grow to cover face

Eccentrically patterned waistcoat

Webley is the eccentric owner of Webley's World of Wonders—a collection of strange alien artifacts, including many alien waxworks. Having become trapped on Hedgewick's World, he is keen to leave, but ends up being partially converted into a Cyberman.

### WEBLEY

The Cybermites attempt to convert the Doctor into a Cyber-Planner, but the process ends up giving him a split personality. Both the Doctor and his ruthless alter-ego, Mr. Clever, decide to play a game of chess, agreeing that the winner will gain total control of the Doctor's mind.

During the Cyber-Wars between humanity and the Cyberiad, the Cybermen built a bunker on Hedgewick's World. They then repaired critically damaged units there, using the visitors to the amusement park as spare parts.

Combat clothing disguises true identity

### CYBERMITE

The Cybermen once programmed miniature metallic Cybermats to carry out certain tasks, such as spreading plague or draining enemies' energy supplies. On Hedgewick's World, however, they use swarms of much smaller cybernetic insects called Cybermites which can partially convert people into Cybermen and also upgrade themselves.

### CYBERMAT

Emperor Ludens Nimrod Kendrick, also called Longstaff 41st, escapes to Hedgewick's World to hide from the pressure he faces as the defender of humanity. Known simply as Porridge, his real identity is eventually revealed, and he must face the responsibilities that come with his august positon—including deciding to activate a bomb to destroy the three million Cybermen, along with the entire planet of Hedgewick's World.

### PORRIDGE

# WEEPING ANGELS

**W**EEPING ANGELS ARE ALMOST as old as the universe itself. They feed off potential energy by sending people into the past. Confined to history, their victims live out their lives. In the present their victims are dead, and the Angels feast on the days they might have had there. The deadly Angels are quantum-locked—they are free to move when no one can see them—and, so, they can easily go by entirely unnoticed.

A touch from an Angel's hand is perilous

Placid pose, with eyes, fangs, and teeth hidden

Angelic appearance frequently found in graveyards

## Sally Sparrow

When photographer Sally Sparrow breaks into the creepy old house Wester Drumlins to take some atmospheric pictures, she discovers the Weeping Angels. Many people have disappeared near the house, having fallen prey to the Angels. One of their victims is the Doctor, stranded in 1969 with his companion Martha Jones.

## Alien Assassins

The moment a Weeping Angel is seen, it turns into harmless stone. In this observed state, the Angels are harmless, but if their victim so much as blinks, the Angels are set free to attack. The Angels move incredibly fast—they can cross a room in the blink of an eye, and that's only about 250 milliseconds!

Sally peels back the wallpaper in the house to reveal a message from the Doctor—addressed to her! She's alarmed, but it takes more messages before she is ready to believe that someone is speaking to her from the past.

### KATHY'S LETTER

*Sally Sparrow*

When the Angels zap Sally's best friend, Kathy, back to 1920, she finds a new life in Hull. But before Kathy dies in 1987, she makes her grandson Malcolm promise to deliver a letter to Sally in 2007, explaining her disappearance.

With the help of Kathy's brother Larry, Sally compiles a folder of information for the Doctor. This completes the link so that, in his future, he will be able to communicate with her from the past.

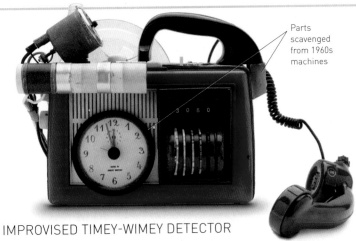

Parts scavenged from 1960s machines

## IMPROVISED TIMEY-WIMEY DETECTOR

The Doctor's homemade Detector can find the Angels' victims by tracking disturbances in time. Designed to go "ding" when it detects anomalies, it also unintentionally boils any egg within 30 paces.

## Tricking the Angels

The potential energy of the TARDIS could feed the Angels forever, but the power released would be enough to destroy the sun. As the creatures from Wester Drumlins surround the TARDIS, hoping to access this energy, it dematerializes, leaving them staring at each other. Constantly observed, this group of Angels will remain stone forever.

## Cherub Angels

The Weeping Angels are constantly adapting. A collection of seemingly innocent Cherub Angels in Julius Grayle's basement are actually baby Weeping Angels—as malicious and hungry as their older, fully-fledged relatives.

In Winter Quay in 1930s New York, some Weeping Angels manage to source enough power to take over the biggest statue around—the Statue of Liberty. Snarling and hungry for time energy, this super army of Angels can be defeated only by creating a paradox in time that wipes them all from existence.

## Angel Collector Grayle

Crime boss Grayle is a serial collector of unusual artifacts that he keeps locked up in the museum in his house in Manhattan. Primary amongst his curiosities are the moving statues he has discovered and deems to be most valuable. He even hires a private investigator to find more of them and source further information.

Grayle summons Angel-expert River Song to provide more insight into his captured creature. Despite its being shackled, it is still not safe for River to get too close. The Angel reaches out a hand and grasps her arm so tight that River must break her wrist in order to escape.

Greedy expression

1930s gangster-style pinstripe suit

JULIUS GRAYLE

## MUSEUM ANGEL

The prize of Grayle's collection is a Weeping Angel that he keeps chained and hidden behind a curtain in his house. To learn more about these creatures that appear everywhere without anybody noticing, Grayle has the Angel tortured to discover whether it can feel pain. Upon looking at its face, River Song diagnoses that it is calling out in distress to its fellow Angels in New York City.

Arm was bound by manacles in Grayle's house

Mouth open wide in silent scream of pain and terror

Body bears scars as lasting sign of torture

# ARMY OF ANGELS

WEEPING ANGELS are the most malevolent and deadly life form ever produced by evolution. These quantum-locked, stone killers feed off the potential life-energy of any being that crosses their path. When the *Byzantium* spacecraft crashes in the 51st century, the Doctor meets a powerful new breed, reenergized by feasting on temporal energy and the radiation escaping from the damaged ship's drives. They have been patiently waiting in hiding to form themselves into a formidable army.

The *Byzantium*, a Galaxy-class starship, can travel for years without stopping to refuel. When a lone Weeping Angel, pulled from the ruins of Razbahan, is transported in the ship's hold, it induces a phase shift in the warp engines. The ship crashes into a site full of hundreds of Angels, all waiting to feast on the ship's massive fuel reserves.

Amy and the Doctor are summoned to the wreck of the *Byzantium* to help Second Class Bishop Father Octavian and his army of Clerics defeat the newly empowered Angels.

## New Super Breed

At the site of the crashed *Byzantium*, there is a crack in the universe, just like the one in Amy Pond's bedroom. It is spilling out temporal energy that the revitalizing Angels there plan to feed on. They think consuming it will give them dominion over all time and space. They do not realise that the power is so strong, it will destroy them and wipe them from from having ever existed.

Serene face masks violent intentions

Angel can control the *Byzantium*'s systems telepathically

### Aplan Mortarium

The crash site of the *Byzantium* is actually an Aplan Mortarium or "Maze of the Dead"—a network of catacombs. It stands on Alfava Metraxis, the home planet of the Aplan race, who were wiped out by the Angels in the 47th century. Under the high-vaulted ceilings are broken statues that are actually starving Angels, desperate to be fed.

Blank page without pictures, because an Angel's image is just as deadly as an Angel itself

Scrawled handwriting, as if written in a frantic hurry

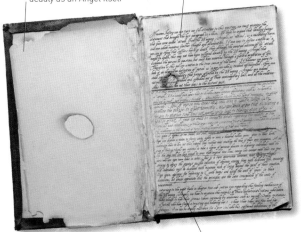

## THE BOOK OF ANGELS

This ancient book is the definitive work and only known book on the Angels, written by a man called Rastan Jovanich. How he knew so much about the Angels is unknown, but possession of that knowledge drove him mad. The book is handed to the Doctor at the *Byzantium* crash site. He keeps it and later stores it in the TARDIS.

Text carries stark warnings

## 51st Century Church

Three thousand years in the future, the Church has become a military unit. Under Father Octavian, twenty armed Clerics are assigned to protect the Doctor and fight the Angels. They are all killed by Angels or by temporal energy spilling out of the crack in the Aplan Mortarium.

The Angels take over the *Byzantium*'s systems, trapping those inside. The Doctor's sonic screwdriver cannot override the Angels' signals, and the Clerics' guns are no use.

Camouflage worn instead of Bishop's robes

### FATHER OCTAVIAN

Eyes are covered to prevent Angel from immobilizing itself by looking at another Angel

Worn-down stone and dull coloring shows Angel has not eaten for centuries

### ERODED ANGEL

When weakened by hunger, Angels wear away, so that they look just as an ancient statue would. This starving Angel has lost most of its original form, including its wings.

## APLAN MORTARIUM ANGEL FACTS

- ■ **Weeping Angels can be very patient for centuries. It doesn't mean that they are dormant.**
- ■ **Rather than just displacing people in time like some Angels, the breed at the *Byzantium* crash site is more violent. They break humans' necks.**
- ■ **Angels can strip the cerebral cortex from a person and reanimate a version of his or her consciousness, in order to communicate with their voice.**
- ■ **As well as killing for the fun of it, Angels enjoy playing with people's emotions, inciting extra fear, anger, or guilt.**

When a person looks at something, it creates a mental image in their brain. In this way, an Angel enters through Amy's eyes and establishes itself inside her mind.

`00:11:27:19`

## Fatal Footage

As anything that holds the image of an Angel will become an Angel itself, the three-second loop of security footage of the Angel in the hold is deadly. Amy freezes the recording on a blip at the end of the loop to render the Angel powerless.

The cruel and mischievous Angels enjoy taunting the Doctor, playing with his guilt over Cleric Bob, a member of the Church that they remorselessly killed. The Angels revel in telling the Doctor that Bob died in fear, after the Doctor had promised Bob that he would be safe.

# THE GREAT INTELLIGENCE

THE GREAT INTELLIGENCE is an evil entity with no physical form. In its endless quest to find a physical existence for itself, it attempts to possess the bodies of other beings. During one such attempt, the Intelligence takes over carnivorous alien snow that can mimic and mirror whatever it finds. When the snow succeeds in creating an ice replica of a human being, the Intelligence believes it now has the blueprint for an army that will wipe out humanity.

## Snow Globe

Awaiting the chance to find a physical form, the Great Intelligence inhabits a large glass globe. It is filled with samples of parasitic snow, through which the Intelligence gathers information about humanity.

## Doctor Simeon

As a solitary young boy who preferred his own company to that of other children, Walter Simeon met a talking snowman, unaware that it was made of parasitic snow that fed on his fear and loneliness. Many years later, Simeon has become a cold-hearted doctor and a servant of the Great Intelligence. He sets up a company called the GI Institute as a front for the entity's plan to conquer humanity.

After scanning the DNA of a governess who died in a tragic accident, the Great Intelligence's alien snow produces a perfect ice version of her body. The ice governess then comes to life and goes on the rampage.

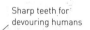
Sharp teeth for devouring humans

## CARNIVOROUS SNOWMAN

The Great Intelligence creates flesh-eating snowmen from living snow. These savage foot soldiers will help it take over the world. Living snow is not frozen water, but is formed from multinucleate, crystalline organisms, which can assume the shape of a snowman within seconds. It also retains a reflection of the thoughts and memories of the people it consumes.

Memory worms are fat alien insects that can wipe a person's memories by touch or biting. When one bites Simeon, his head is rendered empty, leaving it fully vulnerable to possession by the Great Intelligence.

Victorian top hat

Face devoid of emotion

Walking stick wielded as status symbol

## MISS KIZLET

Enslaved by the Great Intelligence at a young age, Miss Kizlet has served her master throughout adulthood. Under its command, she is head of a company that is using wi-fi to upload people's souls to the Internet. The Intelligence then feasts on their minds, growing more powerful in the process.

Brooch with bold design

Professional 20th-century office clothes

## Spoonheads

More formally known as Servers, the Spoonheads are robotic wi-fi base stations. A beam that can absorb the minds and souls of humans shoots out from the back of each robot's spoon-shaped head.

Although a Spoonhead's true appearance is crude and basic, it can disguise itself as a human being by using an image from the subconscious mind of the person it is about to attack. The Doctor is able to hack into this system and create a Spoonhead version of himself, which he then uses to infiltrate Miss Kizlet's computer.

On the 65th floor of the Shard building in London, Miss Kizlet has a wall of screens showing all the people who have been captured and uploaded to the Internet. Each terrified victim repeats the same words over and over: "I don't know where I am."

Miss Kizlet's sophisticated tablet can control the minds of her employees. By moving a slider on the screen, she can make someone more paranoid or more obedient. She can even alter the level of their IQ. In the form of Walter Simeon, the Great Intelligence also uses this technology to communicate with and give instructions to Miss Kizlet.

The Great Intelligence can inhabit any of its Whisper Men at will. When it takes over one of these faceless slaves, the Whisper Man's features quickly morph into those of Doctor Simeon once more—whose form the Great Intelligence continues to use to communicate with others.

On the planet Trenzalore, the Great Intelligence enters the Doctor's time stream, intending to turn all his victories into defeats in order to kill him. However, its plan is foiled when Clara jumps into the time stream, repairing the damage to history and saving the Doctor.

Featureless face

Mouth opens wide to utter Great Intelligence's messages

Funeral clothing echoes outfit worn by Doctor Simeon

## Whisper Men

The Whisper Men are the snarling, blank-faced servants of the Great Intelligence. They get their name from the ominous whispered messages of doom that they bring. Lacking a truly physical form, they are almost ghost-like—their bodies can easily reform when attacked and they can pass their limbs through living beings.

# THE OOD

A HUMANOID HERD SPECIES with squid-like tentacles, the Ood live in telepathic harmony on their snowy planet, the Ood-Sphere. Contrary to popular belief, their kind is not naturally subservient. However, their peaceful existence and their connection to a central hive mind has left them vulnerable to enslavement—under the possession of the Beast on Krop Tor and even at the hands of humans.

Front lobe houses telepathy sensors

Eye turns red with telepathic activity

Translation sphere connects to nervous system and enables the Ood to speak

Coleoid tentacles for feeding

Variety package for translator ball provides different voices

Gloves worn for protection against machine solvents

Ood Operations issued uniform

Boots help Ood keep balance on snow and ice

## Ood Operations

The entrepreneurial Halpen family creates Ood Operations to sell Ood throughout the Human Empire. By setting up breeding farms, they produce hundreds of thousands of Ood servants for the domestic and military markets. The company lobotomizes the Ood into servitude. By the 42nd century, it has convinced all of humanity that the Ood's only goal is to receive orders and that they would die without tasks to perform.

### NATURAL OOD

In their natural state, Ood have two brains. They mainly use the brain in their head, but memory and emotions are processed by the hind-brain, which is held in the peaceful Ood's hands.

Hind-brain

## Ood Operations Slave

Ood Operations cruelly replaces the Ood hind-brain with a translation sphere, which limits the Ood's telepathic ability and cuts it off from the communal Center Brain. This changes the very nature of this gentle species. Natural Ood do not kill. But when the Doctor helps to free them from Ood Operations, the processed Ood begin to experience emotions again – and the anger they feel leads them to destroy their oppressors.

## Mr. Halpen

Ruthless Ood Operations CEO Mr. Halpen is prepared to go to any lengths in order to protect his reputation. When things start to go wrong, he is ready to wipe out every captive Ood in the Ood Operations' factory complex.

## The Center Brain

The telepathic Center Brain connected the Ood in beautiful song for millennia, until Halpen's ancestors discover it beneath the Ood-Sphere's Northern Glacier. Ood Operations keeps it locked up in captivity for 200 years.

Single-dose cup for "tonic"

Supply of Ood-graft hair "tonic" administered to balding CEO Halpen

### OOD SIGMA'S OOD OPERATIONS BELT

Ood Sigma is Halpen's personal servant. The belt is symbolic of a trusted executive slave status.

## Patchwork People

A motley crew of humanoids, including a lost Ood, live on the malevolent, sentient asteroid House—all existing off of the energy it provides. The asteroid itself is a junkyard for old TARDISes that have fallen through a rift in time and space. The so-called "Patchwork People" are servants to House. To prolong their servitude, their body parts are renewed with bits of dead Time Lords.

### IDRIS

Idris is a reluctant inhabitant of House, and she is the only Patchwork Person to not be renewed with foreign body parts. She becomes consumed with the matrix of the Doctor's TARDIS when he is lured to House, and she helps him to escape.

### UNCLE

The darkly sarcastic humanoid named Uncle helps lure more Time Lords to House. His borrowed eyes are thirty years younger than the rest of him.

Loose fabric hides alien right ear

Original body parts

### AUNTIE

Uncle and Auntie work as a pair. Both dependent on House for their existence, they die when he dies. Auntie goes first, followed swiftly by Uncle.

Arm originally belonged to a famous Time Lord

### NEPHEW

The Ood known as Nephew becomes enslaved by House and develops the ability to drain minds and souls. The Doctor is unable to return him to his natural Ood state.

Translation sphere linked to House

# PLATFORM ONE

THE LUXURY SPACE STATION *Platform One* cruises through space between stars. When Rose chooses the future for her first trip in the TARDIS, the Doctor shows off his time-traveling skills by taking her to the year 5.5/Apple/26, five billion years in the future. They arrive on *Platform One* half an hour before the Sun is due to engulf the Earth. They join the galaxy's rich and elite, who have assembled to witness the planet's demise.

Guest list

Guests' names

Touch-sensitive screen

### SPACE PANEL

This electronic device is used by the Steward to check the guest list for the Earth event. It connects with *Platform One's* mainframe computer system, authenticating the guests' identification details.

Solar filters prevent the Sun from burning up everyone inside

Maintenance girders

Disk-shaped hub houses the marble-lined Greeting Hall and other formal rooms

Communications sensors

## Luxury Viewing Platform

Guests can be assured that they will be able to watch the natural phenonemon of the Earth dying in safety and comfort. A force field and solar filters protect *Platform One* from the extreme heat of the Sun, while air conditioning on the space station regulates the temperature inside. All the systems are automatic, run by a huge fan-cooled computer mainframe.

Exo-glass in the viewscreens is capable of self-repair.

The Sun had been threatening to swallow the Earth for years, but the planet was saved by the UK's National Trust. It used gravity satellites to stop the Sun's expansion and restored the planet to its former glory. But when the Trust's money ran out, the Earth was evacuated and left to die. From *Platform One*, Rose's first view of Earth from space is of a dying world.

Blue skin

Formal robe
of welcome

Swept up "bird's nest hairstyle"
is adorned with leaves

Luxurious robe with a
jewel-encrusted collar is
sign of Jabe's high status

Ceremonial
armor of
lacquered
paper

The Trees from the Forest of Cheem
are an arboreal species descended
from the tropical rainforests on
Earth. They are highly intelligent and
have deep respect for all life forms.
As the owners of vast amounts of
land and forests on many planets,
they have great wealth and influence.

Official robes, made
of woven paper and
gold thread

### JABE

A seven-foot-tall alien, Jabe is the
leader of the Trees, visitors from the
Forest of Cheem. This noble, woody
creature has a scanning device that
reveals the Doctor's true identity,
and she sympathizes with his plight
as the last Time Lord.

### COFFA AND LUTE,
### JABE'S COMPANIONS

Helmet and
visor for
protection

Guard's
uniform

Elaborate, flowing dress
hides lianas—retractable,
vine-like appendages

### THE STEWARD

As the manager of *Platform One*, the Steward,
a blue-skinned humanoid, has many duties,
including acting as host, greeting, and announcing
visitors. At first, he thinks that the Doctor and Rose
are intruders, but the Doctor uses his psychic paper
to convince him that he has an invitation. Obedient
to the rules, and very dedicated to his job, the
Steward fastidiously orders that the TARDIS be
towed away for illegal teleportation and issues
the Doctor with a ticket to reclaim it later.

### PLATFORM ONE FACTS

- *Platform One* is owned by a vast intergalactic
corporation, and the galaxy's elite pay to watch
artistic events on the luxury space station.

- Teleportation, religion and all forms of
weapons are forbidden on *Platform One*.

During Earth's
final moments,
*Platform One*'s
shields are
damaged and
the guests are
too concerned
about saving
their own skins
to watch the event
they came to see.

Thousands of blue-skinned humanoid
aliens work as guards on *Platform
One*. One of them, a plumber called
Raffalo, tells Rose that she is from
Crespallion, which is part of the
Jaggit Brocade, affiliated to the
Scarlet Junction, in the Convex 56.
This makes Rose realize how
far away from home she is.

### PLATFORM
### GUARD

# GUESTS OF *PLATFORM ONE*

**W**ATCHING THE DESTRUCTION of Earth from the *Platform One* observation station is a strictly invitation-only event, reserved for the galaxy's wealthy elite. The honored guests, from many worlds and a variety of races and species, have all come to pay their final respects to Earth—and to network with the universe's most influential beings.

Chain of rank

## THE ADHERENTS OF THE REPEATED MEME

The faceless, black-robed Adherents are greeted as guests on *Platform One*. But they are really remotely operated droids controlled by Lady Cassandra. Their gifts of metal spheres contain sabotaging robot spiders.

Vision sensor

Tough metal exoskeleton

## ROBOT SPIDER

The "spiders" are programmed to sabotage the *Platform One* computer, lift the sun filters, and destroy the space station. They come scuttling out of metal spheres passing as gifts from the Adherents.

## THE FACE OF BOE

The sponsor of the *Platform One* event is a huge humanoid head called the Face of Boe. He is the last of Boekind and, at millions of years old, the oldest being in the Isop galaxy. Boe's head is kept in a huge jar, and instead of hair, he has tendrils that end in small pods. This influential alien is one of the few survivors when *Platform One* is almost destroyed as planet Earth explodes.

Face mask provides a special mix of air

Thick, leathery reptile skin

Heavy fur cloaks

Large four-fingered hands with sharp nails

## THE BROTHERS HOP PYLEEN

These two wealthy lizard brothers are from the clifftops of Rex Vox. The pair made their fortune by inventing Hyposlip Travel Systems. They favour fur clothes, which keep their cold-blooded bodies warm.

## CAL "SPARKPLUG" AND GUEST

The cybernetic superstar Cal "Sparkplug" MacNannovich arrives with his "plus-one."

## THE AMBASSADORS OF THE CITY-STATE OF BINDING LIGHT

Oxygen levels must be monitored strictly at all times in these Ambassadors' presence, due to their race's sensitivity to the gas.

Huge feathered head

## MR. AND MRS. PAKOO

These bird-like creatures may be husband and wife, but it is impossible to tell who is who. The pair have huge eyes and vicious-looking beaks. Their feathered heads give away their avian origins, although they walk like humans.

Anti-gravity chair powered by servo-motor

## THE MOXX OF BALHOON

This goblin-like creature's legs are crippled by disease. He travels around on a speedy anti-gravity chair. This device replaces his bodily fluids every 20 minutes because otherwise he sweats dangerous glaxic acid. The Moxx greets visitors with formal spitting.

# LADY CASSANDRA

THE LAST "PURE" HUMAN, Lady Cassandra O'Brien Dot Delta Seventeen, is the only human that hasn't interbred with other species. Being incredibly beautiful in the past, Cassandra was adored by everyone. Now, her desire to keep thin and wrinkle-free means that she is prepared to murder the guests on *Platform One* and cash in on the insurance money to pay for more plastic surgery.

Lipstick and skin are all that are left of Cassandra's body

Skin would disintegrate without constant moisturization

Metal frame connects nerve fibers to Cassandra's brain

Brain kept in a jar of preserving solution

Egg of extinct fire-breathing ostrich

Cassandra gives this rare ostrich egg to the Steward. It actually contains a teleportation field that Cassandra uses to escape from *Platform One* as her plan to blow up the satellite is put into action.

CASSANDRA'S "GIFT"

Lady Cassandra was thought to have died on *Platform One*, but her faithful servant, a forced-growth clone named Chip, hides her brain in a hospital on New Earth. With access to medicine and supplies, he cares for her while spider robots search for a new body.

## Skin Deep

After 708 plastic surgery operations, Cassandra is finally as thin as she always wanted to be. Reduced to a translucent piece of skin with eyes and a mouth, stretched across a frame, she is still obsessed with her looks. Rose is repulsed by her shallowness.

Magnification goggles for seeing the tiniest wrinkle

### PERSONAL ASSISTANTS

Cassandra's personal assistants are always close by, ready to spray her with a scientifically patented moisturizing formula.

In the heat of the near explosion of *Platform One*, Lady Cassandra's skin dries out and explodes. She appears to have died, but her brain survives.

Gloves and masks protect Cassandra from germs

Moisturization formula canister

Canister can be filled with acid and used as weapons

## CASSANDRA FACTS

- Cassandra's "pure" human parents were the last to be buried in Earth's soil.
- She was born an American male but was surgically transformed into an English woman.
- She has been married several times.

# THE SLITHEEN

THE LUSH, ABUNDANT planet of Raxacoricofallapatorius, on the edge of the Milky Way, is home to a species of green-skinned, calcium-based bipeds. While most Raxacoricofallapatorians are peaceful and law-abiding, one particular family's criminality has given the entire species a bad reputation: the Slitheen clan. Banished from their own star system, the Slitheen now terrorize other worlds—including Earth.

Poisonous fingertips

Extraordinary sense of smell can locate fellow Slitheen across vast distances and even detect deaths of loved ones

Eyes blink from side to side

Auxiliary tendon supports long arm

Compression field collar acquired through criminal contacts

Excess skin folds tightly during compression process

Wide foot supports huge body mass

## Second Skins

As wanted criminals on many worlds, the Slitheen are often forced to work in disguise. Earth-based Slitheen use compression field-generating neck collars to squeeze their huge bulks into the empty skin vessels of their human victims. However, gas exchange during compression causes painful flatulence and they find human skins cramped, preferring their "naked" form.

The Slitheen family thinks nothing of profiting from planetary war. On Earth, family members stage the crash-landing of a spaceship in order to kick-start a nuclear war and turn the planet into radioactive slag, which can then be sold in other galaxies as spaceship fuel.

The Slitheen fitted their human costumes with zips, hidden under hairlines or hats. Unzipping produces a burst of contained compression energy.

## Well-adapted Lifeforms

Raxacoricofallapatorians are well suited to life on their own planet. They use their powerful arms to swim from island to island in the great burgundy oceans, and their large eyes pierce through blizzards at the four poles. Forced to abandon this world, one clan poses as influential humans in the British government, seeking war for their own ends.

## RAXACORICOFALLAPATORIAN FACTS

- Raxacoricofallapatorian society is organized entirely around its large, powerful families.

- Family names are a complex affair, with any number of hyphenations expressing the exact branch and sub-branch of complicated family trees.

- The Slitheen is one of the planet's oldest families, tracing its line back to the legendary Huspick Degenerate scion, who controlled an illegal spice-smuggling organization.

## Fatal Weakness

Raxacoricofallapatorians' living calcium structure is highly vulnerable to certain substances, most dangerously acetic acid, which almost always causes a fatal explosive reaction. On their home planet, the most heinous criminals were executed by being lowered into vats of acetic acid, ensuring a slow, painful, melting death.

## Slitheen Lifecycle

The Slitheen, like all Raxacoricofallapatorians, hatch from eggs, using their powerful claws to break through the shell. The TARDIS reverts the Slitheen criminal Blon back into an egg in order to return her to her home planet and give her a second chance to live a better life.

## Attack on Parliament

The closeness of the Slitheen clan is its undoing when all the Earth-based members hold a triumphant family gathering in 10 Downing Street in their natural form. Given a single, reasonably contained target, the Doctor decides to risk launching a Harpoon missile.

## The Abzorbaloff

Originating on Raxacoricofallapatorius's sister planet Clom, the creature known as the Abzorbaloff can absorb other creatures in order to steal their knowledge and consciousnesses. The process is highly unstable and requires a limitation field device to avoid the remnants of the most recently absorbed victims, pulling him apart from the inside.

Faces of absorbed victims remain visible in flesh

Cane contains limitation field that stops Abzorbaloff from being absorbed himself by trapped consciousnesses

The Slitheen named Blon Fel Fotch Pasameer-Day Slitheen impersonating Margaret Blaine of MI5 broke rank with the family and teleported away from the Downing Street blast using a teleporter device hidden in her earrings. She vowed revenge on the miserable human race.

# SATELLITE 5

ORBITING EARTH in the year 200,000, the Satellite 5 space station is the planet's largest media hub. Replacing all earlier broadcast satellites, it transmits news and entertainment throughout the Fourth Great and Bountiful Human Empire. The space station is also home to thousands of human employees, including journalists, who collect the news remotely via neural implants, and the Editor, who oversees them. Also onboard is the Jagrafess, a gigantic slug-like alien, who secretly manipulates the news in order to turn humans into slaves.

In a media centre on Satellite 5, journalists use the chips in their heads to gather news stories from across the Empire. They send the news via data hand plates to Cathica, a journalist implanted with an infospike in her forehead. She lies on an infochair and processes the news before transmitting it to the Empire. However, unknown to the journalists, the news is really going to the Jagrafess for editing before transmission.

## The Editor

The mysterious, softly spoken, and ruthless Editor manages the space station from Floor 500. Unseen and unknown, the Editor monitors the journalists' thoughts via the chips in their heads. He was appointed by a consortium of interstellar banks, who installed the Jagrafess to profit from humanity's enslavement.

Biogenetic analyzer

Data defragmenter breaks down news for transmission

**DATA HAND PLATES**

### CLIPBOARD

Media center seating system

Clipboard's infopaper displays data

### CURRENCY STICK

A currency stick is used like a credit card aboard Satelllite 5. It can be topped up with currency at onboard credit terminals.

Chip inside interfaces with pay stations

An infospike is a portal installed in the forehead that connects the brain to Satellite 5's computers. The infospike opens with a click of the fingers and connects to the computers via spheres of energy in the media centers.

## The Freedom Foundation

The Freedom Foundation is a group of 15 humans who discover Satellite 5's manipulation of humanity and are determined to stop it.

Eva Saint Julienne, using the alias Suki Macrae Cantrell, is the last surviving member of the the Freedom Foundation. Her comrades have all been eliminated. On Floor 500, she pulls a gun on the Editor, but she is killed by the Jagrafess.

Safety catch

Standard P9 phasic barrel

Secondary barrel fires XJ7 microplosives

Semi-organic polymer grip molds itself to user's hand

**FREEDOM FOUNDATION P9 5 PISTOL**

### Freedom Foundation Manifesto

• **Closure of Satellite 5**

• **Full investigation into Satellite 5's activities**

• **No individual to own more than three media outlets**

• **Freezing of the assets of Satellite 5's backers**

## Space Station

Satellite 5 functions as a regular working media hub—except for one section, which has been secretly modified to accommodate a highly unusual occupant: the Jagrafess. This gigantic creature lives on Floor 500, the topmost floor of the orbital platform. Since the Jagrafess's fast metabolism produces massive amounts of heat, a secondary ventilation system and auxiliary heat sinks were introduced to vent heat away from Floor 500. This has resulted in the top floor icing up like an Arctic winter, while the floors below are unbearably hot.

Excess heat vent

Medium range antenna

Fusion generators

Docking ring

Floor 16, the non-emergency medical center

Floor 500 media center is occupied by the Jagrafess and the Editor

Floor 247 specialises in lifestyle programming

TARDIS lands on Floor 139 next to a fast food joint

Main residential floors

Array of signal receivers

Main transmitter broadcasts 600 channels across the Empire

## The Jagrafess

The Jagrafess's full name is the Mighty Jagrafess of the Holy Hadrojassic Maxarodenfoe. The Editor calls him Max for short. This monstrous, slimy alien with razor-sharp teeth is the true ruler of the Empire.

Holographic screens monitor Satellite 5 activity

Keyboard for manual entry

Chairs for the drones who operate the terminals

Floor 500 media center

## Floor 500

Floor 500 media center is the control room of Satellite 5, where the Editor and the drones monitor all human activity on the space station. Everyone who works on Satellite 5 wants to be promoted and transferred up to Floor 500. However, those who make it to the top floor don't live long. Killed by the Jagrafess, they work on as his drones—puppets controlled by the chip in their heads—until their bodies wear out.

# THE SYCORAX

THESE SKINLESS HUMANOIDS orginated on a barren asteroid named the Fire Trap in the JX82 system. Consisting of many warlike tribes, the Sycorax fight with swords, whips, and their own school of magic spells and curses. To survive, these interstellar scavengers ransack other planets. One tribe, the Halvinor, crash through Earth's atmosphere, planning to steal its land and minerals, but don't anticipate encountering the regenerating Doctor when he takes Rose home for Christmas.

## Sycorax Great Hall

This enormous hall was hollowed out of the Fire Trap's core many centuries ago. Its primitive structure is combined with space-age technology, such as a teleporter to travel on and off the asteroid. The hall is used for tribal meetings and the hole in the roof lets in solar and lunar light for ancient Sycorax rituals.

The Halvinor Sycorax ship is an asteroid fitted with powerful engines taken from an alien ship that collided with them. It is used by the Sycorax to raid other planets for food and resources. As the ship moves to attack Earth, it is powered by an All Speed Inter-System Type K engine.

The devastating effect of the Sycorax whip is seen on the prime minister's aide, scientist Daniel Llewellyn.

## Sycorax Leader

It took two and half centuries for the Halvinor Leader to become head of his tribe. He rose through the ranks by various trials of strength and combat, and leads the blood-controlled invasion of Earth.

Thong conducts huge energies

Handle contains micro-fusion generator

Trophy from previous battle

### SYCORAX WHIP

The Sycorax whip, when used on a human body, instantly destroys all the atoms of human flesh, so that only a pile of charred bones remains.

# Fierce Warriors

The Sycorax adhere to traditions of honorable combat and will never turn down a challenge. They are naturally well-equipped for battle: part of the Sycorax skeleton lies outside the skin, covering the top and sides of the head and leaving the lower part of the face exposed to the elements. This exoskeleton, which can be smooth or jagged in texture, resembles a fearsome helmet.

Claw of pet Razorback

Fearsome bone helmet

Blood mane from leader's first kill

Trophies of conquered species

The Sycorax use ancient technology in order to take over worlds. When an Earth probe containing A+ human blood crashes into their ship, they feed it into a control matrix and enslave everyone on Earth who has A+ blood.

Forearm guard

Judoon-skin belt

Lanyard of the order of Prokraxis

Red robe signifies high rank

Protective Baltaric spats

Plumage of Courage

Pommel embedded with precious stones

## SYCORAX SWORD

Barbed handle

Weapons like this sword, along with primitive-looking knives and spears, are adorned with trophies from battles won. They look simplistic, but are nonetheless effective in battle.

The Doctor challenges the Sycorax Leader to single combat for the fate of Earth. Honor-bound to accept, he is defeated by the Time Lord and the Sycorax agree to leave humanity alone.

# NEW EARTH

**T**WENTY YEARS AFTER the Doctor and his companion Rose watched the Sun expand and obliterate Earth, revivalists were inspired to seek a similar world. The ideal place was found and named New Earth 50,000 light-years away in galaxy M87. The Doctor takes Rose there in the year 5,000,000,023, and visits again with his companion Martha 30 years later to see how, if at all, humanity has advanced.

Fluted cap worn by all Sisters

Cat-like features

## Sisters of Plenitude

New New York's hospital is run by the humanoid feline Sisters of Plenitude and their controlling leader, Matron Casp. They specialize in treating incurable diseases, and their reputation for almost-miraculous cures is well-known. The sisterhood is as single-minded about its mission to cure patients as it is fiercely secretive about its treatment methods.

Dazzling New New York—the fifteenth since the United States' original—is New Earth's major city. It is ruled by the Senate, who live in the gleaming Overcity, while the poorer citizens live in the grim Undercity below.

### MEDICAL SCANNER

Display of patient lifesigns

Menu navigation

Position adjustment control

### NEW NEW YORK'S HOSPITAL

In the year 5,000,000,023, a hospital commands an imposing coastal position on New Earth. Its gleaming, sterile wards are sealed from the outside air to prevent contamination. Visitors are disinfected when they enter the building's elevators.

Universal symbol for hospital

Ambulance landing bay

Landing area for non-emergency vehicles

## Human Farm

Deep in the basement of the hospital is the secret of the Sisters' healing powers. Human clones are infected with every known disease and experimented on to find new cures. When the Doctor and Rose discover the clones are sentient, they free them, and a new human species is born.

## The Undercity Motorway

By the time the Doctor returns in 5,000,000,053, life in New New York has drastically changed. Many denizens of the Undercity have set off on the Motorway, dreaming of a better life higher up. This highway is 20 lanes across and 50 lanes deep. Its traffic moves five miles every 12 years, but is going nowhere because the exit has been sealed to protect it from danger above.

Holographic presenter Sally Calypso's fabricated broadcasts convince the Motorway residents that all is normal in New New York.

Communicators, self-replicating fuel, muscle stimulants for exercise, and waste products recycled as food mean no one has to leave their car. Even babies are born onboard. Valerie and Thomas Kincade Brannigan's litter of kittens are Children of the Motorway, and have never known any other way of life.

Fur turning gray with age

Gun carried in case of Motorway pirates

Functional buttons

Decorative design adds color to plain gray uniform

### NOVICE HAME'S BRACELET

Novice Hame's bracelet is actually a teleportation device, and also controls external lights.

## Macra

The giant, crab-like Macra were once the scourge of galaxy M87. They forced humans to mine the poisonous gas they fed on. Over billions of years they devolved into simple beasts and were kept in the New New York Zoo. Escaped specimens have bred and now thrive beneath the smog-shrouded Motorway, hunting its travelers.

## Novice Hame

Catperson Novice Hame nurses the Face of Boe as penance for the Sisters of Plenitudes' clone experiments. She is there when a virus kills everyone in the Overcity, and the Face of Boe hastily seals the Undercity, using his life-force to protect them and keep it running for 24 lonely years. She is also there at his death, but first, they happily see the Doctor rescue the Undercity population.

# THE WEREWOLF

EVERY FULL MOON, cattle on the moors around the Torchwood Estate in Scotland are ripped apart. Locals speak of a giant wolf-like being, and boys vanish without a trace. The clue to these strange events lies nearby in St. Catherine's Glen monastery, where an alien, able to take werewolf form, landed centuries ago and now survives in a succession of human hosts, provided by the monks. When the alien hears that Queen Victoria is visiting the area, it sees its chance to seize power in England by invading her body.

The Torchwood Estate is a place of legend and mystery. Its very name is said to derive from the wood of a lightning-struck gallows—torched wood—used in its construction. Wild rumors were further stoked in the 1800s when the house's eccentric owner, Sir George MacLeish, built a gigantic rooftop observatory.

Landing in Scotland in 1879, the Doctor meets Queen Victoria on her way to Balmoral Castle. Unable to resist the opportunity to make the acquaintance of an English monarch, the Doctor uses his psychic paper to supply him with credentials to tag along to Torchwood House, where the Queen intends to spend the night.

### MISTLETOE NECKLACE

The monks craft mistletoe necklaces to ward off the Werewolf.

## FIGHTING STAFF

Rare wood grows locally

Mistletoe worn around neck under robe

Habit conceals orange fighting robes

FATHER ANGELO

## Bedeviled Brethren

At the monastery of St. Catherine's Glen, the monks, led by the crazed Father Angelo, have come to worship the power-hungry alien that fell to Earth close to their home in the 1500s. They are even willing to kidnap boys from the local village to provide the alien with the human hosts it needs to survive.

In the Torchwood House cellar, Rose finds a strange caged prisoner that the monks have placed there. To her, as a seasoned space-time traveler, its eyes betray the unmistakable presence of a life form that is not from Earth.

Before the Queen and the Doctor arrive at Torchwood House, the monks take over the house, overpowering and imprisoning the staff using their impressive martial arts skills.

Informed of Queen Victoria's movements by the monks, and desperate to infect itself into a being of real power, the alien commands the monks to transport it—in its human host—to Torchwood House. All it needs is for the full moon to provide the power to transform it to its werewolf form.

Sharp claws rip prey apart

Super-sensitive ears

Inhuman eyes betray alien presence inside

## Royal Secrets

Official records remain silent on the strange events at the Torchwood Estate. Yet it is perhaps no coincidence that shortly afterward, Queen Victoria secretly established the Torchwood Institute to research and fight Britain's enemies "beyond imagination."

ROYAL ATTACHÉ CASE

Official emblem of state

Lock is sign of top secret contentst

QUEEN VICTORIA

Sharp teeth rip apart flesh

Thick skin deflects bullets

Powerful hind legs allow short bursts of fast running or jumping

In the rooftop observatory at Torchwood House, there is a telescope with an unusual array of prisms. As the current owner, Sir Robert, is obsessed with werewolf legends and the heavens. The Doctor speculates that these prisms might have a secret function.

## Prowling Beast

To locals, the Werewolf is simply a creature of terror. But the Doctor recognizes it as a lupine wavelength haemovariform—an alien species that requires the specific wavelength of bright moonlight to change its form.

Objective lens cell

Tube ring

Focusing knob

Eyepiece

CENTRAL TUBE OF TELESCOPE

## Light Weapon

Just as the alien needs moonlight to transform, the Doctor realizes that too much light can kill it. He deduces that the prism array in Sir Robert's telescope can project a super-intense beam of light, powerful enough to destroy both the alien parasite and, tragically, its innocent human host.

Unwilling to break through a door smeared with mistletoe, the Werewolf reveals an odd weakness—fear of the parasitic plant.

# GELTH

PITY THE GELTH! These formless creatures have been trapped in a gaseous state ever since the Time War, but they long to have physical existence again. An advance party of Gelth make their way to 19th-century Cardiff where they ask a young girl for help. But it soon becomes apparent that the Gelth have an ulterior motive for seeking a physical form.

Blue eyes turn red once the Gelth are through the Rift

Form changes when Gelth cross the Rift

## The Rift

The city of Cardiff is the location of a weak point in space and time. Known as the Rift, it is where connections are formed with other eras and places and is the cause of the many ghost stories circulating in the area. Having grown up on the center of the Rift, servant girl Gwyneth has become part of it. It has given her "the sight"—the ability to read minds.

The Rift is weakest at 7 Temperance Court, home to Sneed and Co. undertakers. Here, the Doctor communicates with the Gelth via psychic Gwyneth. He allows them use of the corpses, just until he can find them a new home.

## Walking Dead

Decomposing human bodies at the funeral parlor produce gas, which forms the perfect home for the gaseous Gelth. When they animate cadavers, the Gelth stimulate the human's dead brain so the corpse becomes aware of details of its former life.

## Bridge Between Worlds

When the truth is revealed—that there are billions of Gelth and they plan to take over Earth—Gwyneth, who is their link across the Rift, sacrifices herself by blowing up the room full of gas.

## GELTH FACTS

- The Gelth need a gaseous atmosphere to survive—19th-century gas pipes provide an ideal environment.

- It takes three months of hijacking Sneed's corpses before the Gelth manage to communicate their request to Gwyneth at a seance.

- Without a proper bridge across the Rift, the weakened Gelth are only able to inhabit corpses for short periods of time.

- The Doctor agrees to help the Gelth animate human corpses temporarily, intending that he would later help them find permanent bodies elsewhere.

# KRILLITANES

A COMPOSITE RACE, the carnivorous Krillitanes pick the best physical elements from the creatures they conquer, and incorporate them to create an improved form. When the Doctor first met the race, they appeared human, apart from having very long necks. But the next time he encounters them, they have become bat-like.

Wings can lift considerable weight

The Krillitanes have had wings for nearly ten generations, ever since they invaded the planet Bessan, where they killed a million of that planet's winged species in one day.

Jaws ideal for eating children

Claws can rip flesh

## Bad Bats

The Krillitanes resemble bats in more ways than just their wings. They sleep hanging upside down and have very sensitive hearing, which means that they dislike loud noises. Their slim, sinuous bodies are capable of great feats of strength.

### BROTHER LASSAR

A Krillitane named Brother Lassar takes on the human form of Mr. Finch, principal of Deffry Vale High School. Twelve other Krillitanes impersonate staff at the school, aiming to harness the brains and imaginations of the pupils in order to crack the Skasis Paradigm—which would give them control of time, space, and matter.

The Krillitanes cannot change their physical appearance like shape-shifters, but they can use a simple morphic illusion to cloak themselves in human form. However, it takes barely a moment to shrug off their disguise, should they need to make a flying getaway.

### KRILLITANE FACTS

- When there is no fresh flesh to feed on, the Krillitanes sustain themselves with vacuum-packed rats.
- The Krillitanes use Krillitane oil to enhance the intelligence of the pupils under their control.
- Due to overuse and continued physiological alterations, Krillitane oil is now toxic to them.
- As well as physical attributes, the Krillitanes steal technology from other races, such as the means to create a deadlock seal.

# SS MADAME DE POMPADOUR

THE SS *MADAME DE POMPADOUR* is one of the great energy trawlers of the 51st century. Purposed to retrieve dark matter energy deep in space, it was originally crewed by humans assisted by clockwork repair robots. However, when Rose, Mickey, and the Doctor arrive onboard in the TARDIS, the robots are the only life form left. Programmed to repair the ship at all costs, the robots used parts of the crew to fix the ship when it was damaged in an ion storm.

## Energy Trawler

In the 51st century, humans are dependent on dark matter to fulfill their energy needs. Dark matter is an invisible form of energy that is only identified by its gravitational effects. Until it and its computer is damaged, the SS *Madame de Pompadour* is perfectly equipped for collecting this dark matter: rotating arms scoop it up out of space, and it is then stored in the ship's central hub.

Forward rotational arm

Crew's quarters half way along each arm

Dark matter storage

Central hub for dark matter intake

Forward correctional rudder and axis finder

Outer rotational regulator housings

Human eye replaces camera lens

Optical cable

### SECURITY CAMERA

The repair robots are not programmed to feel sympathy and so use the crew's human body parts in whatever ways they can. However, the patched-up ship is useless without a functioning computer.

POWER FEED

Beating human heart pump

Necklace is a gift from the King

## Madame de Pompadour

Living in 18th-century France, Madame de Pompadour was given her formal title by the French king, but was commonly known as Reinette. The repair robots believe that because she is their ship's namesake, her brain will fix their broken computer. Unbeknownst to Reinette, these robots are mercilessly hunting her down by punching holes in the universe, creating time windows through to Earth. They are searching for a window that will lead them to Madame de Pompdadour's 37th birthday, when she will be the same age as the ship.

Using their ship's powerful, undamaged warp engines, one of the robots' time windows eventually opens to reveal a ballroom in 18th-century Versailles. Without these portals, the droids have no way of fixing their ship and therefore no reason to carry on existing.

Wig typical of those worn at French court

Mask conceals clockwork head

## SS MADAME DE POMPADOUR FACTS

- The ship's arms generate an artificial gravity field, as well as a negative magma field that drives the ship forward.

- The ship boasts antiquated sigmus-style warp engines in case its other power sources fail. These are used to create the windows through time and space.

## Clockwork Repair Robot

Although their costumes and masks give them the appearance of French courtiers, a loud ticking noise reveals the repair robots for what they truly are. To match the time zone they have entered, the robots have attempted to disguise themselves accordingly. Each deadly android has a sharp blade hidden in its sleeve, can read humans' minds, and even teleport short distances.

When the repair robots anesthetize Rose and Mickey and strap them to surgical gurneys, it looks like they, too, will be integrated into the ship's systems.

The repair robots contain 51st century clockwork technology. Old-fashioned, reliable Swiss clockwork techniques are integrated with sophisticated space-age computer chips.

Using the fireplace portal, the Doctor first meets Reinette as a child and saves her from the clockwork "monster." She calls him her "fireplace man" and holds onto the belief that he will rescue her when she needs help. When the Doctor accesses the same portal seemingly a few minutes later he is surprised to discover that Reinette has grown into a beautiful young woman. To the Doctor, time passes much more quickly than for Reinette.

The repair robots are able to scan Reinette's mind to work out when her brain is "complete." The Doctor uses telepathy to find out what the robots are looking for but he is shocked when Reinette is also able to read his mind, presumably due to her exposure to his Time Lord abilities, and discover the secrets of his lonely childhood.

Sharp, retractable blade

Silk stockings cover mechanical legs

REPAIR ROBOT

SANCTUARY BASE 6
SCHEMATIC

- CORRIDOR
- AIR SHAFTS
- POWER CONDUIT

Toby's quarters
Command Center
Bore Hole Room
Rocket
Ood Habitation

# THE BEAST

BENEATH A DRILLING STATION on a planetary exploration base, an ancient, trapped evil called the Beast is stirring. Scripture from a pre-human civilization marks the walls, and the planet is orbiting a black hole—going against the laws of physics. The base's crew is drilling to the center of the planet to harness the mysterious power that keeps it in orbit, but as they mine, it becomes clear that the source is more terrifying than they could ever have imagined.

## Base Floorplan

One of many identical bases used in deep space exploration, Sanctuary Base 6 is constructed from pre-fabricated kits. Separate segments allow the oxygen field to be contained in different parts of the base, and areas can be sealed off in the event of a hull breach. This enables the team to enact "Strategy 9"—sheltering in a locked-down safe area and opening the base's airlocks, sucking invaders into space.

Somehow, the planet is generating enough power to keep it in perpetual geostationary orbit around black hole K37 Gem 5. The Doctor calculates that such a power would need an inverted self-extrapolating reflex of 6 to the power of 6 every 6 seconds—a theoretically impossible figure.

## Command Center

The central desk of the command centre controls all the base's essential functions, including the oxygen field, internal gravity system, and rocket link. From here the captain tracks everyone's location from their biochip signals. Overhead shields can be opened to monitor black hole activity.

Halogen light
Used air exhaust
Reinforced plastic visor
Audio pickup
Radio comlink
Air-tight helmet seal
Oxygen hose

### SPACE SUIT HELMET

Protective space suits and helmets must be worn on the surface because the planet lacks atmosphere and gravity. At night, the drills are shut down by the maintenance trainee, and the base's computer shuts off access to the surface.

-00373
-00.7
091%

Screens inside the command center monitor the mining capsule's rate of descent into the mineshaft.

## Drilling Platform

The planet's solid-rock crust is excavated with robot drills and the base crew painstakingly cut a mineshaft 10 miles beneath the surface in a bid to reach the planet's mysterious energy source— an energy giving readings of over 90 Statts on the Blazen scale. The enslaved race, the Ood, does all the dangerous maintenance work on the drilling platform.

Black hole
Sanctuary Base 6
Drilling platform
Capsule
Drilled mineshaft
Gravity globe
Carved monolith of demon
Seal over trap door
Starlight shines through pothole

The horrific monster facing the Doctor is the empty body of the Beast. The Doctor uncovers him when he investigates the Base's power source, and has only seconds to destroy the planet and foil the Beast's escape.

The Doctor
TARDIS

# The Perfect Prison

The Doctor realizes that the planet is an ingenious prison. If the Beast escapes from the pit, the energy source keeping the planet in orbit will collapse, and the planet will be sucked into the black hole. The air in the pit was supplied by the Beast's gaolers so a traveler could stop the Beast's escape by smashing the power source.

## Sealed Trapdoor

Two stone monoliths, standing guard before a circular seal set into the floor, are revealed to be a trap door. Sensors indicate that the Base's power source lies beneath. Without warning, the cavern shakes as the trap door's segments slide back to reveal a deep, black chasm. A voice booms from the darkness: "The pit is open and I am free!"

Ancient drawings

## CAVE MARKINGS

The voice of the Beast tells the Doctor of a people called the Disciples of Light, who rose up against him in a time before the universe was created—something the Doctor finds impossible to believe. As if in confirmation of the devil's words, the Doctor finds cave drawings recording a victory over the Beast and his imprisonment in the pit.

## Ancient Creature

A vast cavern beneath Sanctury Base 6 forms the prison home of the Beast—an ancient creature akin to the devil. The proximity of the people drilling above it has meant that it has easily been able to possess some of their minds—such as crewmember Toby Zed—in a bid to escape.

# RACNOSS

THE ARACHNID-TYPE ALIEN Racnoss are born with a raging hunger, and will devour anything, from people to planets. In the Dark Times, near the beginning of the universe, the Fledgeling Empires went to war against the ravenous Racnoss, wiping them out—or so it was thought. One group managed to escape, but the energy emitted by their ship exerted such a gravitational pull that passing rocks began to mass around it, gradually forming a planet—Earth—and leaving the fugitive Racnoss survivors trapped in their ship at its center.

## The Empress

The Empress is not just the leader of the Racnoss, but is also their mother, as all Racnoss have hatched from her eggs. By reviving the Racnoss hibernating in the Earth's core, the Empress will be freeing her children, who will then be able to satisfy their hunger with human flesh! But her plans are foiled by the Doctor. When he tries to bargain with her by offering the Racnoss safe passage to a new home, she rejects his proposal, condemning her entire race to extinction, as she and the newly awakened Racnoss are then all wiped out.

## RACNOSS FACTS

- Each Racnoss can produce miles of strong, thick protein strands that are used to form webs and bind their prey.

- The Racnoss can hibernate without sustenance for billions of years, but when they stir, they are ravenous.

- The Racnoss have mastered teleportation, so do not need to land their ships on the planets they wish to visit.

## Webstar of Wonder

A star-shaped object blasting bolts of deadly electricity from its eight "limbs" spreads terror as it flies over London's streets on Christmas Eve. This is the Webstar ship of the Racnoss Empress, which had been hiding undetected at the edge of the universe. Racnoss technology is powered by Huon particles that were long ago destroyed by the Time Lords for being too dangerous—but reactivated by the Empress in her mission to free the rest of her kind from within the center of the Earth.

"Crown-like" bone structure denotes imperial Racnoss

Blade-like arms slice through prey

Tough outer skin is shed when outgrown

Pedicle enables free movement of thorax

Spinnerets at base of abdomen produce web strands

# PLASMAVORES

PLASMAVORES ARE AN alien species who live off the vital life-juices of other creatures. While necessary to their survival, blood-sucking is also an addictive pleasure, and many Plasmavores travel the universe searching for rare species to sample. This mania for blood can lead to psychosis and a severe disregard for the lives of others.

### Drone Bodyguards

The Plasmavore calling itself Florence Finnegan is guarded by two Slab henchmen disguised as motorcycle couriers. These basic slave drones are genetically reared for combat and strong-arm work.

Motorcycle helmet masks Slab's real face

Mr. Stoker, one of the specialists at the hospital, becomes an unwitting blood donor when Florence needs human blood in order to escape detection by intergalactic police.

Motorcycle gear stolen from blood victims soon after Florence landed on Earth

Faced with capture by interplanetary police, Florence uses her criminal knowhow to turn an MRI scanner into a lethal weapon. She resets the machine's magnet to send out a massive magnetic pulse that will fry the brainstems of all other living things within a 200 – 50,000 mile (320 – 80,000 kilometer) radius—leaving her unharmed.

A simple bendy straw is used by Florence to suck up the hospital's blood supplies

### Plasmavore in Hiding

Plasmavores are shape-changers who can assimilate the genetic material of any species whose life-juice they drink. One such Plasmavore has taken on the persona of frail 70-year-old Florence Finnegan in the Royal Hope Hospital in order to hide on Earth. "Florence" is on the run from intergalactic law enforcers, the Judoon, after murdering the Child Princess of Padrivole Regency Nine on a whim.

# THE JUDOON

THROUGHOUT THE UNIVERSE, police authorities come in many shapes, sizes, and species. One of the most feared is the private paramilitary security force organized by the thick-skinned, twin-horned species called the Judoon. Each Judoon police officer has the power to administer swift justice: he can arrest, charge, judge, sentence, and execute a suspect in a matter of seconds.

## Hired Thugs

Judoon police have a reputation of being little more than hired thugs. Their methods are certainly authoritarian and brutal, and carried out without emotion. They focus only on their objective and let nothing stand in the way of their justice being done. As they say, "justice is swift." Among other clients, the Judoon enforce laws for the intergalactic regulatory body, the Shadow Proclamation.

Ears with selective hearing

Small eyes betray no emotion

Magnetic seal activates when pressurized helmet is worn

Military fastenings

Language identification scanner

Twin horns for intimidating suspects

Thick skin impervious to most forms of attack

Decayed teeth due to poor diet

Powerful lungs ensure long-lasting stamina

Voice emitter for use when battle helmet is worn

Bulletproof armor padding

Armored wrist guard

Weapons and equipment attached to utility belt

## BATTLE ARMOR, WITH HELMET, SIDE VIEW

The Judoon's battle armor provides maximum impact protection and functions as a pressurized life-support system for use in toxic environments or on planets with non-breathable atmospheres.

Battle helmet with breathing equipment

One-way viewing slit

Thick soles provide protection on uncertain terrain, including toxic spills

Distinctive boot fastenings – Judoon are said to sleep with their boots on as a sign of their dedication to the job

Holster for blaster

Memory chips hold most known languages

Studded kilt is a symbol of a warrior in Judoon culture

Reinforced knee guard used offensively and defensively in combat

Elaborate military boots

Bioengineered metal plates reinforce boots, adding extra power to bone-shattering kicks

## JUDOON BLASTER

Muzzle guard

Cooling unit

Trigger

Blaster gas cartridge chamber

Igniter pin

Grip for Judoon hand

Power cell housing

## SPECIES SCANNER

Indelible branding tip

DNA scan emitter

## LANGUAGE IDENTIFICATION SCANNER

Judoon police carry high-powered blasters, which they are empowered to fire at their own discretion. A single blast of the energy beam can obliterate a person in a flash. Judoon also carry various scanners that allow them to identify and catalog suspects by species. Another scanner can sample and assimilate the languages of most known species—ensuring that the Judoon's orders are clearly understood.

Although the Judoon have no official jurisdiction over Earth, this does not stop them from attempting to capture a Plasmavore suspect hiding on the planet. They use an H2O scoop to suck an entire Earth building onto the surface of the Moon, where they do have authority.

## JUDOON FACTS

- The Judoon are organized along military lines, with troops led by commanders.

- The Judoon travel in gigantic tube-shaped spaceships. Originally built as military battleships, these intimidating vehicles were chosen by the Judoon for their ability to strike fear in others.

- The Judoon's sense of justice has led them to fight both for and against the Doctor. They are among the army that imprisons him in the Pandorica in order to save the universe, but at the battle of Demon's Run, they are outraged by the theft of Amy Pond's baby and come to his aid.

# THE CARRIONITES

MOTHER BLOODTIDE

LILITH

Face can transform into that of a beautiful human

Wrinkled skin of the eldest Carrionite

Spread "wings" of cloak help witch float in the air

A T THE BEGINNING OF the universe, foul witch-like creatures known as the Carrionites flew the skies of the Rexel Planetary System. They used special powers that were derived from the manipulation of specific words to dominate the universe. When the infinitely powerful elemental beings the Eternals discovered which words could control the Carrionites, they banished them to the Deep Darkness. The Carrionites remained trapped in their prison for millions of years.

## Toil and Trouble

The Carrionite wraiths long to escape and take over a world for themselves. They possess the power to harness the energy of strongly expressed emotions and plan to use this skill to pull themselves out the Deep Darkness. Tuning into the intense grief and near madness expressed by the famous wordsmith William Shakespeare when he loses his son, they exploit the energy they derive from this source to try to break free. Three Carrionites escape by this means and are drawn to Shakespeare on Earth in 1599.

Carrionites use a special magical science, based upon the power of words, in their attempts to control people and establish a new Empire on Earth. It closely resembles witchcraft, and employs formulae made out of significant words and shapes to exert its power.

The Carrionites' cauldron is used to communicate, to view the past and to brew potions. The fumes from the witches' brew can control a man's actions, without him being aware of it.

A broomstick aids a Carrionite in her flight, although she is able to fly without one.

Along with their word-based science, Carrionites use a crystal ball to control events on Earth. The are eventually trapped in it by the Doctor.

MOTHER
DOOMFINGER

Finger can kill
with a touch to
the chest

The Globe Theatre was built with
fourteen sides to match the Rexel
Planetary Configuration. The
theater's architect, Peter Streete,
was influenced by the Carrionites
to design the building this way, so
it would be the perfect shape to
act as a portal for
their escape.

Billowing black robes
resemble a crow
when in flight

Carrionites can kill by using
a poppet—a simple doll
resembling their intended
victim. Stabbing the poppet's
chest stops the victim's heart,
and breaking the poppet in
two ensures the victim's
death. By attaching a lock of
a victim's hair to a poppet, a
Carrionite can then control
the victim completely.

Roughly
formed
humaoid
shape

POPPET

## Jail Breakers

When the Carrionite-inspired last lines of Shakespeare's play
*Love's Labour's Won* are spoken, the Globe acts as an energy
converter, opening a portal to the Deep Darkness and releasing
all the Carrionites from their prison. Only Shakespeare—with a
little help from Martha—can find the words to close the portal
and send the Carrionites back to their eternal jail.

## CARRIONITE FACTS

- **All Carrionites are female.**

- **Carrionites try to keep their names secret.
  They can be harmed when addressed by
  their true name. However, this works only
  once. On all subsequent occasions, this
  has no effect.**

- **When a Carrionite forges a link with a
  victim's mind, she is able to see through
  his or her eyes.**

- **Until the Carrionites appeared on Earth in
  1599, many races—even the Time Lords—
  thought they were a myth.**

Shakespeare has met the Doctor
before, but the playwright does not
recognize him because he has
since regenerated.

# THE FAMILY OF BLOOD

THE FAMILY OF BLOOD are alien predators with an acute sense of smell, whose life span is only three months. In their natural form, they are merely balls of gas, but they are able to take the bodies of other intelligent beings and gain their strength and physical abilities. However, these feeble forms are soon expended, so they are seeking the Doctor's body, which will give one of them the many lives of a Time Lord.

The TARDIS chooses to hide the Doctor in 1913 among the pupils of Farringham School. The boys are being prepared for war, but when the Family comes, they take up arms earlier than expected.

## Family of Mine

The Family's bond is strong and the nameless aliens refer to themselves only in terms of kinship: Father of Mine, Mother of Mine, Son (or Brother) of Mine, Daughter (or Sister) of Mine. Son of Mine is the natural leader and favored child—he is the one for whom the Family seek immortality.

## Body Snatchers

When their hunt for the Doctor brings them to England, each Family member takes on a human shape. The mind of each victim is entirely consumed—memory traces may survive, but not enough to enable the Family to pass as their assumed species without arousing suspicion.

A vortex manipulator stolen from a Time Agent allows the Family to track the Doctor. Once on Earth, their spaceship is concealed by an invisibility shield.

Schoolboy Jeremy Baines's body becomes the human host for Son of Mine. Jeremy is fetching illicit beer from Blackdown Woods when he stumbles across the Family and fatally decides to investigate.

Martha suspects something is wrong with maid Jenny at Farringham School when she agrees to share a teapot of gravy. Jenny was snatched by the Family's scarecrow soldiers and consumed by Mother of Mine.

## THE FAMILY FACTS

- The Family's strong sense of smell is just as keen within their human bodies. Yet it can be fooled by olfactory misdirection, or "ventriloquism of the nose," an elementary trick of the Doctor's.

- Family members communicate telepathically. In moments of extreme trauma, they feel each other's pain.

- The laser gun is the Family's weapon of choice. It shoots energy bolts that disintegrate its targets instantly.

The scarecrows, who have been turned by the Family into moving soldiers, are sent to locate a body for Father of Mine. They find Farmer Clark in his field at Oakham Farm.

Little Lucy Cartwright is happily walking along with her balloon when the scarecrows take her. She is the perfect host for Daughter of Mine.

**MOTHER OF MINE**
Gaseous form enters human through eyes

**SON OF MINE**
Pupil's body allows access to Farringham school

**DAUGHTER OF MINE**
Childlike appearance disarms foes

## FATHER OF MINE

Respectable appearance allays human suspicion

## Scarecrow Soldiers

Scarecrows are not uncommon in rural Herefordshire, England—but these scare more than just crows. Son of Mine fashions rough humanoid shapes out of inanimate materials to create a scarecrow army. He gives them basic motor and sensory abilities using the process of molecular fringe animation.

"Eyes" allow limited vision

SCARECROW SOLDIER

Clothes keep straw in humanoid shape

Following the Family's orders, the scarecrow foot soldiers march inexorably toward the schoolboys' guns. Straw men feel no pain, but they are unable to mend themselves if they lose their humanoid form.

The Doctor goes to great lengths to make himself human to hide from the Family, not just for his sake, but also to protect them from punishment at his hands. But when the Family tracks down the Doctor and threatens the village, Martha—helped by psychic schoolboy Tim Latimer—has to bring the Time Lord back before the Family causes any more deaths.

Straw filling provides bulk of scarecrow

Shoes give firm base for straw-filled legs

## Eternal Life

The Family wanted to live forever, so the Doctor, left with no alternatives by their actions, makes sure they do. Father of Mine is trapped eternally underground, wrapped in unbreakable chains that were forged in the heart of a Dwarf Star.

Inside every mirror, occasionally glimpsed but rarely fully seen, is Daughter of Mine. She can never leave her looking-glass prison, where the Doctor visits her once a year.

The Doctor tricks Mother of Mine into the event horizon of a collapsing galaxy. She is drawn irresistibly into an inescapable black hole, through which she will fall, screaming, for all eternity.

Son of Mine is suspended in time in a living death, eternally aware but unable to move. The Doctor puts him to work as a scarecrow, guarding the fields of England forever.

# THE MASTER

THE MASTER WAS one of the Doctor's oldest friends, but he became his most bitter enemy. They attended the Time Lord Academy together, but eventually both tired of Gallifreyan life and became exiles. The Master's evil schemes were frequently foiled by the Doctor, and he met his final end when he was sucked into the Eye of Harmony in the TARDIS—or so the Doctor thought.

Respectable appearance conceals a psychopath

## Hidden in Time and Space

The Master used up all of his lives pursuing diabolical schemes and the Doctor's destruction. However, during the Time War, the Time Lords remembered the Master's battle mania and resurrected his body so that he could fight alongside them. Instead, he ran away scared, eventually reaching the planet Malcassairo where he hid as Professor Yana.

## Professor Yana

To escape the ravages of the Time War, the Master hides himself as a human called Professor Yana at the end of the universe. Using techniques similar to those used when the Doctor became human in order to escape the Family of Blood, the Master's transformation from Time Lord to a human is total.

Gallifreyan children are made to stare into the Untempered Schism, a gap in the fabric of reality. The sight sent the Master mad, filling his head forever with the pounding sound of drums.

Laser Screwdriver is now the Master's weapon of choice

The Master's Time Lord self is contained in a pocket watch that is identical to the Doctor's. A perception filter within the watch prevents him from noticing it and realizing his real identity. On opening it, the Master's biology, personality, and memories return. One heart becomes two, his body temperature lowers, and his respiratory bypass system is restored.

## Restored Time Lord

Professor Yana becoming the Master again reveals the meaning behind the Face of Boe's prophetic "You are not alone" message to the Doctor; the Doctor is not the last of his kind as he previously thought. The restored Time Lord escapes to Earth in the Doctor's TARDIS.

## Harold Saxon

After his release from the pocket watch, the Master arrives on present-day Earth. He assumes the identity of "Harold Saxon." He convinces the world that he is a Cambridge graduate and a novelist who became Minister of Defense. He rose to fame after shooting down the alien Racnoss. He is then elected Prime Minister of Great Britain.

Tip shoots deadly laser beam

Isomorphic controls allow only the Master to use them

### LASER SCREWDRIVER

The Master's laser screwdriver is similar to the Doctor's sonic screwdriver, but its technology is based on laser beams rather than on focused sound waves.

Roedean-educated Lucy Saxon appears to be Harold's devoted wife and companion, but his cruel treatment slowly destroys her, and she is the one who finally shoots him dead.

### SIGNET RING

This ornate ring with Gallifreyan engravings is worn on the Master's right hand. It contains the Master's genetic code and is rescued from his funeral pyre by a woman named Miss Trefusis.

## The Archangel Network

Harold Saxon launches the Archangel Network. This worldwide cell-phone network, carried by 15 satellites, transmits a rhythm that gives the Master hypnotic control over the entire population.

As part of the Archangel Network, the whole of the south coast of England is turned into a rocket shipyard. Rockets are built out of scrap metal by slave labor, in preparation for the Master declaring war on the universe. Each rocket contains a Black Hole Converter.

## The Last of the Time Lords?

When the Master is defeated, the compassionate Doctor will not let him be executed, but knows that the Master cannot be allowed to go free. As the only other apparent Time Lord in existence, the Master is his responsibility—the Doctor plans to keep him in the TARDIS and care for him. But betrayed Lucy shoots the Master and he refuses to regenerate, preferring death to eternal imprisonment with the Doctor. The Master seems to die with no hope of returning, leaving the Doctor believing he is the last of the Time Lords once more.

The distraught Doctor takes the Master's body to a deserted beach, and places it on a funeral pyre.

# THE TOCLAFANE

**P**RIMITIVE CREATURES wired into mechanical shells represent the final evolution of humanity. In the year 100 trillion, the nothingness at the end of time drove humans to regress into these spherical beings known as the Toclafane. They were then rescued by the Master, who transported them back from the future to invade present-day Earth.

The Toclafane are the Master's enforcers, enabling him to cover the Earth in work camps, and churn out rockets for waging war.

Magnetic clamp holds together the outer shell

Lasers disintegrate targets

## The Master's Secret Weapon

Malevolent Time Lord the Master befriends the vulnerable and impressionable Toclafane. Loyal to him without question, they carry out his every destructive instruction. The Master uses them to conquer Earth and enslave the human race—the first stage in his plan to found a Time Lord Empire across the universe.

Merciless killing machines, the Toclafane speed through the air after their victims. They have lasers for long-range attacks and blades for up-close slicing and dicing.

Blades cause extra damage when the sphere rotates

TOCLAFANE SPHERES

Tough metallic shell can fly through space undamaged

Retracted blades and spikes

Human head is wired into the sphere

## INSIDE THE TOCLAFANE SPHERE

The Paradox Machine is a device the Master created by reconfiguring the TARDIS. It forms a temporal paradox that allows the universe to continue, despite an apparent contradiction. The machine allows the Toclafane to kill their ancestors without wiping out their own existence.

Each sphere houses a withered head—the last remnant of the Toclafane's human form. All six billion Toclafane share a collective memory of the final thoughts and experiences of the last humans. They are haunted by the never-ending darkness and cold of the end of time.

## The Utopia Project

In the year 100 trillion, when the universe was coming to an end, the last humans fled the planet of Malcassairo in search of Utopia—a perfect place, believed to have been built by the Science Foundation as part of the Utopia Project in order to preserve humankind. But Utopia was just a myth, and the travelers found nothing but oblivion. Despair led them to evolve into the Toclafane.

Insectoid exoskeleton

Mandibles evolved from insects

Chantho helps the humans to flee Malcassairo by working on the space shuttle as Professor Yana's assistant. She nurtures unrequited feelings for him, quashed when she discovers he is the Master working in disguise.

The spacecraft for the journey used an experimental engine, built using whatever was available to hand, including gluten extract as a binding agent.

### CHANTHO

Chantho is the very last of the insectoid Malmooth race, native to the planet Malcassairo. Malmooth bodies survive by drinking their own internal milk, and social conventions dictate a very polite and fomulaic way of speaking. Chantho's every sentence must begin with "chan" and end in "tho."

## The Futurekind

A fierce humanoid race, the Futurekind were feared to be the final future of the human race. Humanity's actual fate—becoming the Toclafane—was no better. In order to leave Malcassairo, the last humans had to escape the Futurekind.

Billions of Toclafane spill into the sky from the future, programmed to destroy

## Mass Destruction

On the Master's orders, the Toclafane kill one tenth of Earth's population on first contact. Under his regime, they use terror to maintain order among the population, before the Doctor succeeds in returning them to the future.

Sound of drums beats constantly in head

Sense of smell can track the Doctor

Hands ripple with electricity, and can shoot bolts of energy

# THE MASTER RACE

ONE MASTER POSES a serious threat to the universe. But six billion of them would be catastrophic. After the Master was shot by his wife, Lucy Saxon, the Doctor made sure that his body was burned. However, someone stole the Master's ring—containing his genetic code. Through this ring, the Master returns and finds a way to turn every human being into himself, so that he can take over the whole universe.

## Life-giving Elixir

An underground cult loyal to the Master performs a ritual and creates an elixir to bring him back from the dead. The key ingredients for this potion are the Master's ring, the sacrifice of their own lives, and a catalyst unwittingly provided by the Master's former wife, Lucy Saxon—a tissue with an imprint of her lips, which holds his biometric signature.

## A New Body

The Master's body may look the same as when he was Harold Saxon, but it is flawed, because his spurned wife, Lucy, sabotaged the resurrection process. Her actions fail to prevent the Master's return, but do reduce his body's stability. With new supernatural power and strength, the crazed Master seems unstoppable, but he is slowly and surely using up his life force.

## The Immortality Gate

The Immortality Gate is a medical device to cure people by transmitting a template that rebuilds cells. Rather than treating one person at a time, it can cure the populations of whole planets at a time. Driven by the desire to give his daughter immortality, Naismith enlists the Master to fix the machine. However, the Time Lord has his own plans for it.

The Gate runs on nuclear power that is controlled via specialist isolation booths. The feed is manned 24 hours a day and cannot be left unattended: the locking mechanism means that a technician cannot leave one side of the booth until the other side is occupied.

The green-skinned Vinvocci originally built the Immortality Gate, which was later commandeered by billionaire Joshua Naismith. In order to claim it back, two Vinvocci, using shimmer devices to appear human, went to work for Naismith.

## The Naismiths

Joshua Naismith is a ruthless billionaire who owns his own private army and will stop at nothing to get what he wants. His daughter, Abigail, is as vain as he is rich, and both are meddling in alien technology that they do not understand. Joshua is aware of the Master's dangerous reputation, but he arrogantly believes that he can control him.

Body language displays close father-daughter relationship

ABIGAIL AND JOSHUA NAISMITH

## Cellular Transformation

The Master hijacks Joshua Naismith's plan for the Immortality Gate and uses it to turn everyone on Earth into himself. People become not just genetic copies of the Master, but him in entirety. All six billion Masters share the same mind. In essence, the human race no longer exists.

## Heroic Wilf

Wilf was drawn into the world of the Doctor through his granddaughter Donna, and he has his own role to play in saving Earth. The old soldier has one more battle left. He uses his old RAF piloting skills to control an asteroid rocket, ducking and diving the missiles the Master's armies fire at him and the Doctor.

The Doctor's former companion Donna is not affected by the cellular transformation because she is not strictly human after she became part Time Lord in a past incident. However, if she remembers anything about her life with the Doctor, her head will overload and she will die. The Doctor left her with a self-defense mechanism: when her head starts to heat up, she collapses, but remains alive.

TRINITY BEFORE POSSESSION

TRINITY AFTER POSSESSION

## Six Billion Masters

By possessing every politician, soldier, and military leader on Earth, as well as others, such as American newscaster Trinity Wells, the Master gains control of all the planet's resources and weapons. Six billion crazed warmongers now prowl Earth and plan to turn it into a giant warship to wage war across the universe.

Clothes suitable for newsreading role

## Time Lord Pawn

The Master believes that he is now in charge, but he doesn't realize that he is being manipulated. When he finds out that he is merely a pawn in the plans of other Time Lords, he is quick to take his revenge on Rassilon, Lord President of the High Council of Time Lords.

# THE HEAVENLY HOST

**Razor-edged halo can be thrown as weapon**

**Wings stretch out to fly**

ONBOARD THE luxury Max Capricorn Cruiseliner *Titanic*, a group of tourists are served by angelic-looking robots known as the Heavenly Host. En route from the planet Sto in the Cassavalian Belt to Earth to experience primitive cultures, the tourists soon discover that the golden creatures—and things onboard the *Titanic*—are not exactly shipshape.

## Sinking the Ship

Max Capricorn Cruiseliners are advertised as "the fastest, the furthest, and the best." Their *Titanic* was named after Earth's most famous ship and is owned by Capricorn himself. He has a secret agenda to destroy the ship, kill the passengers and crew, and wipe out life on Earth.

Capricorn bribes the dying Captain Hardaker to sabotage the ship to cause it to crash. By magnetizing the ship's hull, it attracts meteoroids, which damage the Nuclear Storm Drive engines and cause the *Titanic* to plummet toward Earth. If the ship hits the planet, the nuclear engines will explode and destroy all human life.

MIDSHIPMAN FRAME

**Metal hand can deliver karate-style blows**

Captain Hardaker has just six months left to live, so feels he has little to lose if the *Titanic* crashes. In contrast, the newly qualified midshipman Alonso Frame is only on his first trip, and, as such, dutifully volunteers to help save the passegers

## Angels of Death

The robotic Heavenly Host's usual job is to provide tourist information and assistance. However, they follow orders from Max Capricorn, and he has reprogrammed them to kill everyone onboard the *Titanic*. When a Host is asked to fix a passenger's necklace, it nearly breaks her neck!

CAPTAIN HARDAKER

**The Host's default position is standing straight, with hands together and head bowed**

When the TARDIS crashes into the ship, the Doctor stows away on board. He realizes that the ship is in danger, but the Host try to stop him from saving it.

## HEAVENLY HOST FACTS

- **Each Host has the strength of ten men.**

- **The Host's robotics can be temporarily deactivated by an electromagnetic pulse.**

- **The Doctor initiates Security Protocol One, which overrides any previous instructions and compels a Host to answer three questions.**

## The Doctor and the Waitress

Astrid Peth dreams of seeing the stars—and the Doctor makes her dreams come true by taking her to the alien planet Earth. He recognizes a kindred spirit in the feisty young waitress, and helps her see that nothing is impossible.

Astrid yearns to travel and see the entire Universe. Before getting her job on the *Titanic*, she spent three years as a waitress at a spaceport diner.

Uniform based on 1920s waitress

Smart tweed suit

Chest replaced by cybernetics following accident

**ASTRID PETH**

**BANNAKAFFALATTA**

**MR. COPPER**

Bannakaffalatta, a Red Zocci cyborg, and Mr. Copper, the *Titanic's* historian, help the Doctor defeat the Host. Bannakaffalatta dies, but his bravery enables the Doctor and other survivors, including Mr. Copper, to reach the safety of Earth.

Head is only remaining organic part

Protective casing contains oxygen field

Closed mouth conceals golden flashing tooth

Device can control the *Titanic's* engines

Life-support system constructed in secret on Max's homeworld of Sto

**MAX CAPRICORN**

## TELEPORT BRACELET

Wrist-worn bracelets like this one can transport passengers between the *Titanic* and Earth.

## LIFEBELT

London is deserted—except for Wilfred Mott and the Royal Family. The Queen escapes just as the Doctor pilots the *Titanic* safely over Buckingham Palace.

## Vengeful Cyborg

Before being ousted by his board and vowing revenge on all those involved, cyborg Max Capricorn ruled his company with a rod of iron for 176 years. He believes that he is the victim of anti-cyborg prejudice and hopes that using the *Titanic* to destroy Earth will ruin the company and land his former colleagues in jail for mass murder. In the meantime, Max has set up offworld accounts and plans to use these secret funds to retire to the beaches of planet Penhaxico Two.

Astrid falls to her death while saving the Doctor. Her molecules are held in stasis and the Doctor sends them to the stars.

# ADIPOSE INDUSTRIES

THE BREEDING PLANET ADIPOSE 3 has been stolen by the Daleks, so the Adipose must find a new way to reproduce. Hired "nanny," Matron Cofelia, needs a planet with high levels of obesity and she finds Earth, where she sets up Adipose Industries. The company's unwitting customers think they are buying a miracle diet product—but really they are forming baby Adipose out of their own flesh!

Observation windows

Hover function enables stationary orbit

## NURSERY SHIP

"Seeding" a Level Five planet like Earth—using it to grow another species—is against galactic law. While the nursery ship collects the newborn Adipose, the Adiposian First Family murders Matron Cofelia to cover its tracks.

One million customers in Greater London sign up to the Adipose Industries special offer: £45 ($75) for three weeks' supply of weight-loss pills, plus a free gift of an 18-carat gold pendant.

## PENDANT

## The Adipose

Formed from human fat, new baby Adipose are created at 1:10am every day. These baby Adipose may appear friendly and sweet, but some of them have already killed, albeit unwittingly. In a crisis, Adipose are programmed to consume their entire human host rather than just their fat.

Capsule bio-tunes itself to its owner so as to affect only that person

The gold pendant may be advertised to new customers as a free gift, but it actually attracts fat, binds it together, and galvanizes it to form a body.

## Miss Foster

Matron Cofelia of the Five-Straighten Classabindi Nursery Fleet adopts the alias Foster when she is employed by the Adiposian First Family to facilitate the birth of a new generation of Adipose. Her devotion to her charges is matched only by her callousness toward the humans she utilizes in her plans. She will kill to achieve her goals.

## FAT-EATING PILL

## WATCH

This wrist watch doubles as a communicator between Miss Foster and her minions.

Miss Foster's pen has similar properties to the Doctor's sonic screwdriver.

## SONIC PEN

### ADIPOSE FACTS

- Each Adipose consists of exactly 2.2 pounds (1 kilogram) of living fat.

- In a crisis, Adipose can form themselves from body parts other than fat, but converting bone, hair, and internal organs makes them sick.

- Newborn Adipose are small enough to fit through cat flaps.

The Adipose Industries building is converted into a Levitation Post, ready to float ten thousand baby Adipose up to the nursery ship.

Although prized as a priceless gem, the Firestar crystal is in fact a Vespiform Telepathic Recorder. It holds the essence of the alien's identity, and can instantly transfer knowledge, emotions, and even a particular mindset to a Vespiform.

# VESPIFORM

THIS ANCIENT AND WISE race of shape-shifting insectoid creatures comes from the Silfrax Galaxy. A lone, curious Vespiform left his hive homeworld to come to Earth in 1885. It took on a human form called Christopher in order to learn more about the human race.

Powerful wing

Giant antenna sense touch, smell, and taste

Compound eye combines multiple angles for wide field of vision

Long legs for landing and crawling

Insectoid exoskeleton

Stinger full of deadly poison

## Giant Wasp

In its natural form, the body of an adult Vespiform is around eight feet (2.4 meters), which makes it a formidable opponent to a human, especially when buzzing with a fierce temper. However, Vespiform biology is susceptible to insecticides such as piperine, found in pepper. Drowning in water is also a real risk as their wings disintegrate and their spindly legs are too weak to swim.

## LADY CLEMENCY EDDISON

Firestar was a gift from Christopher

## An Insect Romance

Shape-shifting Vespiform are able to interbreed with other species. In Delhi, India in 1885, Christopher met British Aristocrat Lady Clemency Eddison. She conceived his child, but not before Christoper drowned in a monsoon, leaving her heartbroken.

Body can take on the Vespiform wasp-like form, when the Reverend is angry

Eddison Hall, home to Lady Clemency, and its estate are passed down the female line, along with the Eddison title.

## Hidden Vespiform

Local village vicar Reverend Golightly was adopted, so he has no idea that he is half-human and half-Vespiform. Vespiform offspring remain in their birth form until a strong emotion breaks the genetic lock. One day in 1926, anger, and the proximity of the Firestar, trigger Arnold's transformation into a poisonous wasp. With his emotions raging, he goes on a murderous rampage.

Reverting to the natural Vespiform state creates a pink-purple haze. This genetic re-encoding also leaves traces of morphic residue—a viscous by-product of the transformation process.

## REVEREND ARNOLD GOLIGHTLY

## STINGER

Loss of a Vespiform's stinger renders it temporarily helpless. However, the stinger can be regrown within hours.

## AGATHA CHRISTIE

In 1926, the well-known murder-mystery writer Agatha Christie disappeared mysteriously for eleven days. Doctors diagnosed amnesia, but some suggest it was a publicity stunt or revenge on her cheating husband—or perhaps the result of an attack by an alien Vespiform.

# PYROVILES

Fiery breath can incinerate humans

Hot stone form can be shattered by cold water

Magma flows through body

Stone exoskeleton

**E**ARTH FEELS THE HEAT when the fire-loving stone Pyroviles wake up! After their escape pod crash-landed on Earth, these alien creatures lay dormant for thousands of years under Mount Vesuvius—a volcano near the city of Pompeii in Italy. In 62CE, an earthquake heralds their awakening. With much of their technology still intact, the Pyroviles plan to return to their planet, Pyrovillia, or alternatively, convert Earth into their new home.

## PYROVILE FACTS

- **While the Pyroviles lay beneath the Earth's crust, their homeworld Pyrovillia was stolen by the Daleks.**

- **Vesuvius's eruption is so powerful that it cracks open a rift in time. Ripples from the explosion radiate back to the start of the Pyrovillian timeline—the earthquake in 62CE.**

The magma creatures travel from the heart of Vesuvius to Pompeii via an underground network of hot springs.

## Reconstituted Rock Creatures

With their original bodies smashed into dust when their ship crashed, the Pyroviles need a new form. Inhaled as tiny particles by the citizens of Pompeii, they then force themselves inside the human brains, where they use psychic talent to bond with their host's body, gradually transforming it into stone.

Pyrovile dust is contained in the vapors from Vesuvius's hot springs, which are breathed in by the mystics of Pompeii, in the belief that it aids their visions.

Inside Vesuvius, the Pyroviles blaze with ideas. Their energy converter will harness the power of the lava in the volcano to create a fusion matrix and speed up the conversion of humans into Pyroviles. In their new Empire, the Earth will burn and the oceans will boil.

Pompeii was a popular holiday destination for Romans, until Mount Vesuvius erupted with the force of 24 nuclear bombs on August 23, 79CE. It's unknown exactly how many of the town's 20,000 inhabitants died, but the scale of the disaster was unprecedented.

## The Sibylline

The name "Sibyl" is given to women thought to be possessed by the god Apollo and thus granted the gift of prophecy. Joining the Sibylline Sisterhood is a life-long commitment and considered a prestigious and honorable occupation for Roman women. They wear painted eyes on their hands as a symbol of their foresight, but stubbornly refuse to listen when Donna Noble tries to tell them about the impending volcanic eruption.

Entire body has become stone

## The Doctor's Dilemma

Pompeii or the world? The Doctor has to choose. Vesuvius's lava will be used up in the Pyroviles' plan, but by stopping the aliens, the eruption goes ahead and the whole of Pompeii is destroyed.

### THE DOCTOR'S WATER PISTOL

The Doctor's pocket water pistol is the perfect weapon to use against the hot Pyroviles. Water causes them pain and makes their molten bodies solidify and then shatter.

Not even the Pyroviles' escape pod could survive the eruption of Vesuvius. But as it is programmed to evade danger, it removes itself from the heart of the volcano and lands safely nearby with Donna and the Doctor.

## The High Priestess

As head of the Sibylline Sisterhood, the High Priestess is highly respected. However, she too succumbs to the Pyrovile dust and begins to speak with the voice of the Pyrovile. Halfway between human and Pyrovile, she thinks that her painful transformation is a blessing from the gods.

### ENERGY CONVERTER

This energy converter is designed to convert humans the world over into Pyroviles. The plans for it came to Lucius Dextrus in a dream inspired by the Pyroviles themselves.

One of six circuits, each carved from marble

Toga conceals stone right arm

## Pyrovillian Prophet

Lucius Petrus Dextrus is Pompeii's Chief Augur—a type of Roman priest. Having inhaled Pyrovile dust, he is slowly turning to stone. The crack in time caused by the eruption gives Pyrovile-infected citizens, like Lucius, the ability to see echoes of the future.

### LUCIUS PETRUS DEXTRUS

## The Caecilius Family

Caecilius is a marble dealer living in Pompeii with his wife, Metella, son, Quintus, and daughter, Evelina, when Vesuvius erupts. History states that those who stayed in Pompeii died. Technically, there is therefore nothing that the Doctor can do to stop Caecilius and his family from perishing. However, Donna encourages the Doctor to look beyond the letter of the law. He can surely save one family without changing history entirely, and so he chooses the Caecilius family.

# SONTARANS

AN AGRESSIVE HUMANOID SPECIES from the planet Sontar, Sontarans care about nothing but war. They have been fighting their deadly enemy, the Rutans, for 50,000 years, and there is no end in sight. Their every action serves to further their cause, whether it's searching for a strategically advantageous position or increasing the number of Sontaran warriors to take part in the conflict. Combat is glorious for Sontarans, and to die heroically in battle is their ultimate goal.

Probic vent is a Sontaran's only weak spot

Staal enlists the help of teen genius scientist Luke Rattigan and his students to lay the foundations of a clone world on Earth. However, he has nothing but contempt for these human helpers and proposes to use them for target practice when their usefulness is at an end.

Three-fingered hands

## General Staal, the Undefeated

General Staal of the Tenth Sontaran Battle Fleet is charged with turning Earth into a clone world to create more Sontaran warriors. When the Doctor disrupts this plan, vengeful Staal prepares to wipe out the human race. He is proud to enter the fray with his troops, and when the Doctor gives him the choice between death or defeat, he refuses to submit, even though it costs the lives of himself and all his soldiers.

## Attack of the Clones

All Sontarans look similar because they are clones. At their military academy on the planet Sontar, one million battle-hungry Sontaran clones are hatched at every muster parade. Under the charge of Sontaran High Command, each warrior is immediately given a rank and dispatched on a battle mission.

Muscles designed for load-bearing rather than leverage

## Commander Skorr, the Bloodbringer

Second-in-command Skorr leads the Attack Squad to Earth, relieved to finally be facing combat. He welcomes his death in battle at the hands of UNIT's Colonel Mace, as an honorable warrior's death, regretting only that he will not see the Sontarans victorious.

Body weighs several tons on the high-gravity planet Sontar

## SONTARAN FACTS

- Sontarans have a strict code of honor. As warriors, nothing offends them more than accusations of cowardice.

- The probic vent on the back of a Sontaran's neck is its major Achilles heel. However, Sontarans consider it a strength as it means they must always face their enemies during battle.

- Sontarans are vulnerable to Coronic acid, which causes a quick but agonizing death in seconds.

## Sontaran Spacecraft

The Tenth Sontaran Battle Fleet consists of a Command Ship and a number of detachable capsules that can be moved into position when Battle Status is enjoined. Sontaran ships are impervious to nuclear missiles and the separate Scout Ships are small enough to avoid detection by radar.

Spherical Scout Ship capsules detach from main ship

**COMMAND SHIP**

Sphere spins through space

Single Sontaran pilot

**SCOUT SHIP**

Point fires a disabling beam that can temporarily render a person useless

Baton emits an energy pulse that can repair systems like teleport pods

**SWAGGER STICK**

The Sontarans' love of warfare drives their desire to invent ever more methods to destroy their enemies. From blasters and beam guns to grenades and gas attacks, the clone warriors have a weapon for every occasion.

Clips onto handheld blaster to make it a rifle blaster

Attaches to Sontaran's belt

**CLIP-ON BLASTER EXTENSION**

Barrel emits laser beams that kill instantly

**BLASTER GUN**

Display indicates power usage

Trigger designed for three-fingered grip

Head exposed without helmet in "open skinned" battle pose

Sontaran blaster gun is never far from Strax's hands

As Madame Vastra's unconventional butler, Strax finds it difficult adapting to a life of servitude. While he accepts Vastra's role as the leader of the Paternoster Gang, he still harbors a healthy mistrust of any being that isn't a Sontaran.

Red light indicates grenade is activated

Activation button

**STRAX'S GRENADE**

This Sontaran grenade is one of Strax's favorite weapons, as it brings the added satisfaction of blowing things up. Strax has little patience for stealth tactics, preferring to engage the enemy directly with every weapon at his disposal— whether they're actually needed or not.

## Nurse Strax

Strax is a disgraced Sontaran forced to work as a nurse during the Battle of Zaruthstra in 4037 as punishment, for crimes he has never confessed. Indebted to the Doctor, who saved his life, Strax later helps his Time Lord ally in the fight against the Headless Monks at Demon's Run. He appears to die a glorious death during the battle, but is brought back to life by Silurian Madame Vastra. What Strax lacks in brains, he more than makes up for with brawn.

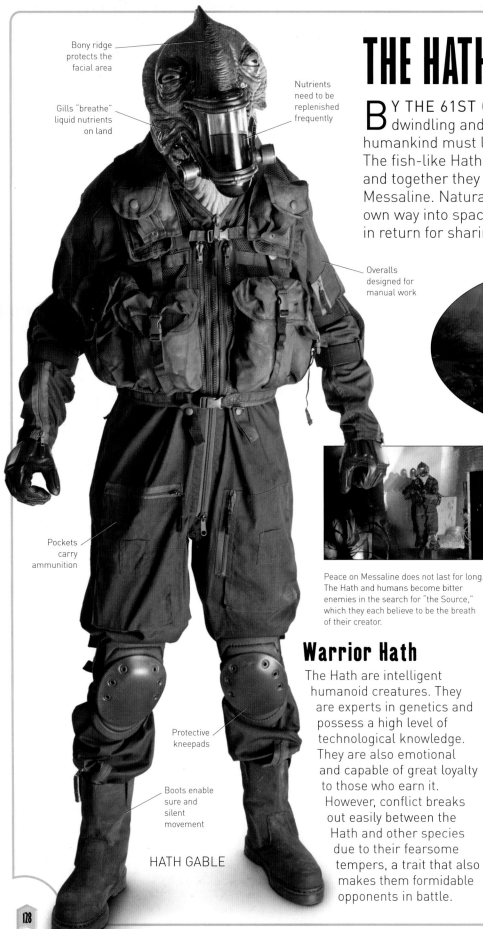

Bony ridge protects the facial area

Gills "breathe" liquid nutrients on land

Nutrients need to be replenished frequently

Overalls designed for manual work

Pockets carry ammunition

Protective kneepads

Boots enable sure and silent movement

HATH GABLE

# THE HATH

BY THE 61ST CENTURY, Earth's resources are dwindling and its population is increasing, so humankind must look for other planets to colonize. The fish-like Hath assist humans in their search, and together they discover a suitable planet named Messaline. Natural pioneers, the Hath made their own way into space before teaming up with humans in return for sharing technology and resources.

Peace on Messaline does not last for long. The Hath and humans become bitter enemies in the search for "the Source," which they each believe to be the breath of their creator.

## Messaline

The three moons of Messaline reveal a barren wilderness of bleak moors and treacherous bogs. The high levels of ozone and radiation make the planet's surface uninhabitable, so the Hath and human visitors must build their colony underground.

## Warrior Hath

The Hath are intelligent humanoid creatures. They are experts in genetics and possess a high level of technological knowledge. They are also emotional and capable of great loyalty to those who earn it. However, conflict breaks out easily between the Hath and other species due to their fearsome tempers, a trait that also makes them formidable opponents in battle.

## HATH FACTS

- Although Hath speech is difficult to decipher due to the bubbling of their nutrient flasks, humans and Hath are able to communicate.

- The Hath have a similar skeletal structure to humans, including ball-and-socket joints in their shoulders.

- The Hath have piscine genes in their ancestry, but technology allows them to live on land. Flasks of the nutrient liquid that they breathe operate similarly to a human's underwater oxygen tank.

## GENERAL COBB

Unyielding mission commander General Cobb leads the human army. His inability to work alongside the Hath triggers a generations-long war between the two species as they quarrel over who should assume control of Messaline. As a result, colonists divide into rival factions.

Holstered gun used in "shoot first, question later" approach

The colonists need extra workers, so the Hath create the progenation machine, which takes genetic material from the original pioneers and uses it to form fully grown beings of the same race.

Two hearts, like a Time Lord

## DETONATOR

Originally designed for building work, this detonator is used as a weapon by the humans.

# Progenation Machine

The humans on Messaline reprogram the progenation machines to create soldiers—embedding military history and tactics in the generations that spring from them. When the TARDIS lands on Messaline, a soldier forces the Doctor's hand into one of the machines. A tissue sample is extrapolated and accelerated, and within minutes the Doctor genetically becomes a father!

# Genetic Anomaly "Jenny"

The Doctor's daughter is genetically a Time Lord, but has been engineered to be a soldier. Donna calls the blond teenager "Jenny" because she is a "genetic anomaly." Despite their physiological likeness, the Doctor claims there is no real relationship between them. However, he grows to care for his "daughter," and Jenny learns compassion and wanderlust from her "father." When she is shot, her Time Lord DNA enables her body to restore itself.

A doctor treats anyone, and when you are a space-traveler, that includes aliens. Martha resets Peck's dislocated shoulder and gains the trust of the injured Hath and his colleagues.

Weapon of Hath design

Super-temp Donna realizes the mystery numbers on the walls are the building completion dates. This means that, despite having been on Messaline for "generations," the colonists have actually been there for only seven days!

Ammunition magazine

## HATH PECK

In return for Martha helping him, Hath Peck bravely insists on accompanying her across the perilous surface of Messaline. He ends up rescuing Martha from a deadly swamp.

# The Source

Tales of the Source have been passed down through generations of colonists. It turns out to be a terraforming machine—a device used to make bare planets habitable. The gases it releases into the atmosphere accelerate evolution on Messaline, rejuvenating the ecosystem, creating abundant plant life and restoring peace between humans and Hath.

# VASHTA NERADA

**B**Y THE 51ST CENTURY, there are many ways to experience narratives—holovids, direct-to-brain downloads, fiction mist—but people still love books. The Felman Lux Corporation creates a planet-sized Library controlled by a computer called CAL. However, the company doesn't realize that the newly printed books have been made from trees containing micro-spores of the deadly alien Vashta Nerada. Over time, more than a million of these microscopic, flying carnivores hatch inside the Library.

## The Library

When the human-hunting Vashta Nerada hatch in the Library, it seals itself, leaving a single message: "the lights are going out." The Library's creator, Felman Lux, cannot decode the seals and enter, but he exhorts his descendants to keep trying and to safeguard CAL.

100 years before the Doctor arrives, the Vashta Nerada enter their deadly hatching cycle. There are 4022 humans in the Library at the time, and nowhere is safe for them to be teleported to, so CAL saves them all to her hard drive.

A group of expeditioners led by River Song venture into the Library, but many fall prey to the Vashta Nerada. The swarms devour human flesh, then animate the remaining skeletons.

## Space Piranhas

The name "Vashta Nerada" means "the shadows that melt the flesh" because they strip their victims to the bone in seconds. They are also known as "piranhas of the air." After devouring one of the visitors to the library, a swarm of the carnivores animate the leftover spacesuit and use its neural relay to communicate a ghostly, deadly message.

### SECURITY CAMERA

### CHARLOTTE ABIGAIL LUX (CAL)

CAL in her original human form

Charlotte watches the Library through living cameras.

## VASHTA NERADA FACTS

- The Vashta Nerada are found on a billion worlds, including Earth, where they live mainly on roadkill.

- The creatures hunt by latching onto a living food source and keeping it fresh until they devour it.

- The tiny beings normally live in the darkness, but can also be seen as the dust in sunbeams.

The Doctor brokers a deal with the Vashta Nerada: he will allow them free reign over the Library for eternity, but in exchange they must give him a day's grace to evacuate everyone trapped on CAL. He plans to sacrifice himself to stabilise the power to CAL, but River Song insists on taking his place.

Book-loving Charlotte Abigail Lux was terminally ill, but her father, Felman Lux, wouldn't let her die. Instead, her mind became the main command node of the Library, which Lux built for her eternal pleasure.

# THE FLOOD

**H**UMANITY'S EXPLORATION of the stars makes a leap forward in the year 2058 with the first human settlement on Mars. The pioneering crew on Bowie Base One studies the planet to see if a colony is viable. They tap into an underground glacier in the Gusev Crater for water supplies, unaware that the water holds a viral life form known as the Flood. A faulty filtration system leads to some of the crew becoming possessed.

## GADGET

Gadget is a robot controlled remotely by special technical gloves. Unlike humans, he can travel unaided on the surface of Mars.

- Monoptic auto-focus infra-red vision
- Probe to collect samples
- Basic memory and processor
- All-terrain caterpillar tracks
- Fully articulated fingers and thumb

Possessed eyes

Strong-minded Captain Adelaide Brooke leads the team on Bowie Base One. She pursued a dream of space travel after she saw a Dalek as a child. Thanks to her intellect and determination, she was the first non-American NASA candidate, the first woman on Mars, and is famous for her research. The Doctor greatly admires Adelaide, calling her the "woman with starlight in her soul."

## Watery Nightmare

Six of the nine crew on Bowie Base One, including Tarak Ital, fall victim to the Flood virus and have their bodies transformed: their mouths crack, their teeth blacken, and their eyes turn a haunting light-blue. Controlled by a hive mind, the zombie-like creatures try to infect the rest of the crew, using them to reach water-rich Earth.

Water drips constantly from the body

The Flood virus spreads through water. Nowhere is safe: water can wait and seep through the tiniest of cracks or build up pressure to break through the strongest of defenses.

## THE FLOOD FACTS

- The Flood virus infects a victim through contaminated water. It possesses and transforms a person's body and mind, leaving no trace of their personality.

- Infected people gush an endless supply of water from their mouths and hands.

- The possessed can survive on the surface of Mars without protective suits or oxygen.

- Host bodies are driven to perpetuate the Flood by infecting more people and hunting out new sources of water.

TARAK ITAL
POSSESSED
BY THE FLOOD

## Self-destruct

When Adelaide realizes that the crew is doomed, she arms the base's nuclear self-destruct to stop the Flood from reaching Earth. Those infected perish in the explosion, but the Doctor steps in to rescue the remaining healthy crew in the TARDIS.

# SAN HELIOS

HALFWAY ACROSS the universe in the Scorpion nebula, the civilization of San Helios has been wiped out by scavenging stingrays who devour everything in their path. And their next stop is planet Earth! All that stands in their way is a handful of passengers on a London bus that has fallen through a wormhole and landed on San Helios. But these are no ordinary passengers—one of them is the Doctor, and he'll do anything to get them all home.

Teeth are capable of eating through anything

Metal exoskeleton can pass through wormhole undamaged

Tail steers when flying

### Lady Christina de Souza

A minor member of the British aristocracy, Lady Christina is bored with her life of privilege. Seeking adventure, she has turned her back on her dull upbringing and become a notorious jewel thief. However, her subsequent adventures with the Doctor bring her far greater excitement than any of the heists she has pulled off.

Stylish, fashionable attire

Close-fitting clothes for ease of movement

Sturdy and silent rubberized boots

Christina uses her wits as an audacious thief. In it for the thrills rather than the money, she swipes the Cup of Athelstan from right under the noses of four museum security guards. Pursued by police, she makes her escape by leaping onto a passing number 200 bus and thus meets the Doctor, a fellow passenger.

The Stingrays have turned San Helios into a barren wasteland in less than a year. All that is left is sand—lots of it! The sand is clogging the bus's engine, its wheels are stuck and it is out of gas. The Doctor calms the panicking passengers and makes them see that they must all work together, if they are to find a way back to Earth.

The bus takes the brunt of the wormhole, protecting the passengers inside like a Faraday Cage

### Bus Detour

One minute, the number 200 is an ordinary London bus, entering a tunnel in traffic. The next, it is battered and stranded on the sandy world of San Helios. It fell through a wormhole, but returning to Earth is not so simple: the driver tries to walk through and is fried to a skeleton.

## Ravenous Stingrays

Body is size of a small car

These scavenging stingrays swarm in their billions and travel from world to world consuming everything in their path. When a planet is stripped bare, they fly in a massive formation, circling at high speed until they rupture space and create a wormhole. Then they pass through to another unsuspecting world and repeat the cycle.

Bones reinforced with metal creature has consumed

Stingrays travel in vast swarms, which look like a sandstorm to the untrained eye. But the Doctor soon realizes that stingrays are approaching, and knows that Earth will be history if they reach the wormhole they created.

Solid gold

## Cup of Athelstan

This cup was given to King Athelstan of England at his coronation in 924CE. Gold is an excellent conductor of electricity, so the Tenth Doctor uses the cup to forge a device to get the bus home—destroying it in the process.

Compound eyes just like flies

Telepathic translator

Mouth sucks up organic waste

Moving mandibles make clicking sounds used to communicate

## Tritovores

Two Tritovores—a race of green-skinned humanoids with heads similar to thoses of flies—are also stranded on San Helios. They arrived in one of their large, hi-tech spaceships, hoping to trade, but soon realized that the stingrays had wiped out all life on the planet. Believing the number 200 bus is a weapon that caused their ship to crash, the Tritovores capture the Doctor and Christina. But they soon realize that the stingrays are responsible and join forces. Unfortunately, before the two Tritovores can reach the bus, they fall prey to a stingray.

Impulse laser pistol

## Scientific Advisor

Professor Malcolm Taylor is a top scientific advisor at UNIT. A computer genius, he devises a program that will seal the wormhole created by the stingrays. Determined to save the lives of all those stranded, he bravely defies orders to use it until the number 200 bus, carrying the Doctor, Christina, and their fellow passengers, is safely back in London. Only after his new best friend the Doctor calls and tells Malcolm to close the wormhole, does he run his program—just ahead of the pursuing stingray swarm.

Tritovores technology is very advanced and the Doctor is pleased to find anti-gravity clamps, which, when attached to the wheels of the bus, help the bus fly home.

UNIT-issued lab coat

PROFESSOR
MALCOLM TAYLOR

## PRISONER ZERO FACTS

- The first time Prisoner Zero duplicates someone with whom it has formed a psychic link, they fall into a deep coma. They stay unconscious until the link is broken.

- Prisoner Zero can create perception filters to stop it from being seen. It can also use them to conceal anything it chooses.

- Multi-forms can live for millennia.

Prisoner Zero is extremely dangerous. Amy narrowly escapes death when she discovers it in her house.

# PRISONER ZERO

A HIGHLY DANGEROUS creature, known as Prisoner Zero, has escaped from an alien police race known as the Atraxi. A crack in space allows the fugitive to flee to Earth where it hides in the house of young girl Amy Pond. The creature remains concealed there for twelve years using its shape-shifting abilities to avoid detection. But it's only a matter of time before the Atraxi locate it— with grave consequences for Earth.

Shape-shifter's natural form

Malevolent yellow eyes have vertical slit pupils

Gelatinous, snake-like body

Internal organs glow below the translucent skin

Mouth has razor-sharp teeth and a ridged tongue

## Escape Route

Prisoner Zero flees through the crack in space and time in Amy's room and creates a perception filter to hide within her house for 12 years. From the other side of the crack, a voice could be heard saying, "Prisoner Zero has escaped." It takes the Doctor's arrival to uncover that the disembodied voice is an Atraxi prison guard, who then warns him that Prisoner Zero is hiding on Earth.

Nurse Rory Williams suspects something is amiss when he sees supposed comatose patients out in the English town of Leadworth. He uses his phone to take photos of them.

## Escaped Prisoner

The escaped alien convict Prisoner Zero is an inter-dimensional multi-form, meaning it can change its shape and even copy the identities of more than one creature at a time. To adopt another form, Prisoner Zero must first create a psychic link with a living, dormant creature, so the patients in Leadworth Hospital's coma ward provide numerous guises for the escapee.

## The Atraxi

The Atraxi are a sophisticated race of aliens that use advanced technology to search for Prisoner Zero on Earth. They scan the entire planet to detect alien life, but miss their escapee because it has taken human form. The fugitive is dangerous, so the Atraxi are willing to destroy Earth to stop it from fleeing. They break Article 57 of the Shadow Proclamation when they surround Earth, seal off its atmosphere, and threaten to boil the planet if Prisoner Zero does not surrender.

Giant eyeball used to see and speak

Ship contains enough firepower to incinerate Earth

Crystalline structure is similar to a snowflake

ATRAXI SHIP

Prisoner Zero bares its teeth when threatened, giving away its true identity.

PRISONER ZERO AS COMA PATIENT AND DAUGHTERS

## Patient Impersonator

Prisoner Zero's psychic link with its victims enables it to take the form of anything the victim dreams about. When Amy and Rory find a terrified mother and her two daughters in the coma ward, Amy soon realizes that they are actually Prisoner Zero impersonating a patient dreaming of her daughters. The shape-shifter's disguise is ruined when it confuses their voices and one of the girls speaks with the mother's voice.

The Doctor tries to alert the Atraxi by using his sonic screwdriver, but it breaks before they detect its signal, so he must find another way to get their attention. Using Rory's phone, he creates a computer virus to reset every counter on Earth to zero.

### RESET CLOCK

Clock counters turned to zero as the computer virus takes hold

With the help of Earth's space and alien experts, the Doctor's reset virus spreads across the world. The Atraxi trace Rory's phone to find the Doctor and Prisoner Zero's location.

## Duplicate Doctor

The Doctor transmits photos of the coma patients on Rory's phone to the Atraxi to identify Prisoner Zero, but it now has a psychic link to Amy. She dreams of herself as a child with the Doctor, so Prisoner Zero impersonates them both. The real Doctor gets her to dream of Prisoner Zero's true form. It is then easily identified and recaptured, saving Earth.

# SMILERS

Demonic red eyes strike fear into the heart of anyone who looks into them

Head rotates to show three different faces: smiling, frowning, and angry

**I**N THE CLASSROOMS, in the elevators, in the streets—the android Smilers are everywhere on the *Starship UK*. As the monumental ship travels between the stars in the 33rd century, Smilers keep watch over the British population, letting them know what is good and what is bad. Any lawbreakers discover that the smiling law enforcers have a very nasty side to them!

MANDY

Young schoolgirl Mandy explains to the Doctor and Amy about the Smilers and life on *Starship UK*.

Long purple robe hides a mechanical body

## Terrifying Presence

The Smilers are an extension of the *Starship UK*'s security system, observing life and activity onboard in an attempt to maintain order. The British people live in fear of them: no one walks too near their booths, and while the starship is battered, untidy and filthy, the Smilers' booths are spotless—kept clean by frightened citizens. It's one more clue that something is not quite right about life on board the ship.

Onboard the *Starship UK*, people travel by Vators. These are vast elevators operated by Smilers that travel through district blocks.

The Smiler's face is happy and placid, as long as citizens obey the rules

## SMILER FACTS

- The Smiler androids are self-repairing and if damaged can return to full working order within minutes.

- There have been Smilers mounted in booths on the *Starship UK* since it left Earth in the 29th century.

- Everyone onboard *Starship UK* is terrified of the Smilers. They don't go near them or their booths if they can help it.

SMILER BOOTH

Plaque on the booth reads "Smiler"

Smilers are located all over the *Starship UK* in specially designed Smiler booths. People know whether their behavior meets with approval or not from the expression on the Smiler's face. If displeased, a Smiler can open the front of its booth and step out in order to deal with lawbreakers.

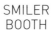

A frown is a warning that laws are being broken, and that bad behavior must cease.

This feared expression is a final warning before punishment is meted out.

# Liz Ten

Liz Ten is really Queen Elizabeth the Tenth, supposed ruler of the *Starship UK*, which, in actuality, is controlled by the government. She is about 300 years old, but her body clock has been adjusted, so that she lives the same ten years over and over again, making her effectively immortal. She is unaware of all this, as at the end of each ten-year time block, her memory is wiped clean.

## Winders

The Winders are the police force of the *Starship UK*. They wind up the Smilers and are the only people to know the terrible truth about the *Starship UK*—that it's not a working spaceship at all but a ship built upon a suffering Star Whale. They take an oath to keep this secret and they uphold the tyrannical system that stops people from asking questions.

The Winders are so devoted to serving the *Starship UK* system that they have become cyborgs—part human, part Smiler.

Ring contains knock-out gas

Wind-up key

Winders wear long dark robes with hoods that conceal their "Smiler" side until they choose to reveal it.

Porcelain mask allows Liz to walk inconspicuously among her subjects

### WIND-UP KEY BOX

Key

On the *Starship UK* many things, such as the street lamps, are wind-up operated. The Winders patrol the streets and have keys for all of them.

Shape is perfectly molded to face

Mainspring provides power, when wound up with the key

### LIZ TEN'S MASK

### WINDER

Gun barrel

Energy blast converter

Sighting

Energy focus

Isomorphic trigger

Liz Ten's gun fires energy blasts that can stop the formidable Smilers, but only temporarily because they are able to repair themselves.

Battery compartment in grip

### LIZ TEN'S GUN

On/off switch

High-definition display

Camera

Eternal momentum battery

Liz Ten communicates with her government officials through her PDA. The high-tech device can also be used to track people. Liz gives her PDA to the Doctor to track Amy, who's been kidnapped by Smilers. Finding the PDA later abandoned, Liz tracks the Doctor with it.

Sumptuous red velvet cape is a clue to Liz's regal identity

Gold plating

### LIZ TEN'S PDA

Wireless connector

# STAR WHALE

WHEN EARTH WAS being devastated by solar flares, the planet's nations fled to the stars—all except for the United Kingdom. Hearing the cries of the country's children, a Star Whale arrived to help them. However, the creature's kindness was mistaken for a lucky coincidence and the beast was captured by Britain's leaders. They built a ship upon its back and cruelly forced it to carry the nation through space.

Each massive tower block houses an entire county

### Gentle Giant

Star Whales are giant alien creatures with several flippers and tentacles that trail behind them. They also have numerous tendrils along their chins and undercarriages. Over the years the Star Whale population has declined—in fact the one carrying the *Starship UK* is the last of its kind.

### Friend Not Foe

In the Tower of London, where the Star Whale is "piloted," Mandy and Timmy see a huge tendril emerge from a hole in the floor. They learn that it is part of the Star Whale. Instead of attacking, it strokes them affectionately. Amy sees this and pieces together the clues: the creature is ancient, kind, and hates to see children harmed—it deliberately came to Earth to try to save them and didn't need to be coerced into helping.

### Dinner Time!

After the Doctor presses the "Protest" button in the voting booth, the floor below disappears and he and Amy fall down into the Star Whale's mouth. To escape, the Doctor makes the monster vomit—it's not dignified but it works!

The Doctor had been unable to detect an engine on the *Starship UK*. After landing in the monster's mouth, he finally understands how the spaceship flies without one.

## STAR WHALE FILM

Voting booths are equipped with monitors, showing a film about the capture and enslavement of the Star Whale that carries *Starship UK*.

## Voting Booth

In the name of democracy, every five years people over the age of 16 find out the truth about the *Starship UK* in a film shown to them in voting booths. Afterward, they are given a choice: to protest about what they have learned or to forget it. Most choose to forget; those who protest are fed to the beast.

Like her subjects, Liz Ten is shown the truth about *Starship UK*, but every ten years instead of every five. As Queen, she must choose to forget what she has been told or abdicate by pressing the appropriate button in her voting booth. Every time she has chosen to forget.

### FORGET BUTTON

### ABDICATE BUTTON

At Winder Division 1, the Winders and Hawthorne, *Starship UK*'s head of government, watch the citizens—and the Queen herself—on huge television monitors as they vote.

The exterior of the *Starship UK* was designed with an extended shelf to conceal the Star Whale below it

## The Driving Force

Builders of *Starship UK* didn't understand the benevolence of the Star Whale and thought it would only carry them under duress. They accessed the Star Whale's brain and blasted it with energy bolts to make the creature fly faster. This cruel practice has been taking place ever since.

## STAR WHALE FACTS

- Star Whales communicate using sounds that are too high pitched for the human ear.

- According to legend, Star Whales helped the first human space travelers to navigate their way through space safely.

- Star Whales are bioluminescent creatures and have glowing spots on their tentacles and tendrils.

# SATURNYNES

ONE WOMAN AND THOUSANDS of her male children are the only surviving members of a race of vampire fish fleeing from their planet of Saturnyne, lost through a crack in space and time. The woman and her eldest son settle in 16th century Venice as humans named Rosanna and Francesco Calvierri. They establish a desirable school for young ladies, the House of Calvierri, and plot to restore their race. Meanwhile Rosanna's other children are lying in wait in the canals.

## Vampiric Fish

The vicious Saturnynes are amphibious anthropod aliens who need constant hydration when on land. In their natural form, behind their perception filters, they have four insectoid legs and a thick tail. With their razor-sharp teeth, they feed in swarms like piranhas.

Respiratory system can both breathe air and extract oxygen from water

Razor-sharp teeth for tearing through flesh

It would be easy to mistake the Calvierri girls for vampires with their fangs, aversion to sunlight, and the fact that mirrors don't show their reflections. In fact they are worse—Saturnynes. A perception filter manipulates the brainwaves of anyone looking so they see humans. Their fangs cannot be hidden because self-preservation overrides the mirage, while their brains become confused by mirrors, causing the absence of a reflection.

Scales overlap downwards to reduce drag in the water

Isabella's dowdy clothes from before joining the House of Calvierri

Legs sprout from the abdomen, rather than the thorax, like Earth's insects

## Aristocratic Aspirations

Impoverished 17-year-old Isabella joins the House of Calvierri at her boat-builder father Guido's urging, in the hope that she will gain a better position in society as a result. When she goes out walking beneath a perception filter and doesn't recognize him, Guido becomes convinced that something sinister has happened.

Isabella betrays the Calvierris by helping the Doctor to escape from them. She pays for her treachery with her life—she is fed to the Saturnynes in the canal.

ISABELLA

Multi-jointed legs end in bladelike bones that pierce prey

# The House of Calvierri

Rosanna Calvierri is a fearsome matriarch who carries the sole responsibility for ensuring the future of her race. She is converting the girls at her school into Saturnynes by drinking their human blood and replacing it with her own. Her hope is that they will become suitable mates for her male children. Her son Francesco is a ferocious predator with a cruel streak, but he is also fiercely devoted to his mother.

Calvierri coat of arms bears a fish emblem

Control hub for elements manipulator

## Alien Technology

Rosanna receives visitors to the palatial House of Calvierri while sitting on a grand throne. It is a symbol of her opulent life, but the intricate gold work and rich velvet also hide advanced Saturnyne technology. The chair is the control hub for a complex system of circuits that can manipulate the weather.

### CALVIERRI THRONE

Orbs open to reveal controls

### FRANCESCO CALVIERRI

Reticella lace ruff reflects fish quills of natural form

Opulent attire denotes wealth and stature

### ROSANNA CALVIERRI

Crustaceous exoskeleton molts as the creature grows

Broad tail helps keep heavy body stable on land

When on land, body needs constant hydration

Rosanna can control the weather with this elements manipulator, situated on the spire of the House of Calvierri. It forms dark clouds, creates rain, and causes the sky to boil. It can whip up storms violent enough to trigger earthquakes and tidal waves that will swamp Venice.

Device is disguised as decorative sphere on building spire

Two halves of orb close to conceal the inner workings

With a flick of a switch on a high-speed rotating cog, the Doctor ends the storm and saves Venice.

### ELEMENTS MANIPULATOR

On/off switch hidden on cog

Wheels and spheres rotate around the central spike

Rosanna uses her influence in Venetian society to seal the city under the pretense of protecting it from the Plague. She plans to use the elements manipulator to sink Venice, kill all its human inhabitants, and create a new Saturnyne colony.

When Rosanna fails to ensure the future of her race, she jumps into a canal in human form and is devoured by her children. The Doctor tries to save her, but she is determined to die.

# SILURIANS

LONG BEFORE HUMANS evolved, a humanoid reptilian race called Silurians ruled Earth. When an apocalypse was predicted, the Silurians retreated deep underground to hibernate until it was safe to return to the surface. In the meantime, evolution moved on and now human beings believe they own Earth. The Silurians disagree, but have also become divided amongst themselves.

## SILURIAN FACTS

- Silurians are cold-blooded reptiles who bask in the heat from the Earth's molten core.
- The Silurian race went into hibernation when they thought a planet was going to smash into Earth. This planet entered Earth's orbit and is now known as the Moon.
- Silurian activity underground releases mineral traces that turn the grass on the surface blue.
- The creatures have built an ingenious transportation system harnessing geothermal currents that pass through tunnels.

In the Welsh hamlet of Cwmtaff, a patch of blue grass has led a scientific research team to drill deep into Earth's crust. Since this project began, strange things have been happening: bodies vanish from graves, pets go missing, and steam pours from holes in the ground. Continued drilling reveals the perpetrators to be the Silurians, awakening within their vast underground city.

## Silurian City

Bathed in an orange glow from the Earth's molten core, the Silurian city spreads majestically over a wide valley. Buildings hewn from rock and granite are sealed together with cooled lava. The settlement has its own self-sufficient ecosystem, processing carbon dioxide and providing food. Geothermal power is used to split water from deep-crust minerals into hydrogen and oxygen, which is stored in pockets above the city for a fresh air supply.

## Eldane

Old and wise, Eldane is the tribal elder of the Silurians. Like the Doctor, Eldane sees the potential for good in humanity and believes homo sapiens and homo reptilia can live peacefully side-by-side. But his argument that the military's role is to protect not provoke falls on deaf ears.

Eyes are wizened with age but still sparkle

Leader's ceremonial robes

### MALOHKEH

Malohkeh, a brilliant scientist, has been monitoring changes to life forms on Earth's surface for 300 years, while his fellow Silurians sleep. Driven by the quest for scientific discovery, he has no sentimentality toward the creatures that he studies and torments—including humans—but he doesn't intend them any malice.

## Family of Fear

Mo Northover works on the drilling project at Cwmtaff. Along with his wife, Ambrose, and son, Elliot, he is astonished to discover the existence of the Silurians. When Ambrose's father is injured by the Silurians and Elliot is kidnapped, they display the worst of human nature and respond with violence. Their fear and anger is born out of love and desperation to protect their family, but it derails the peace process.

Family gathers in a protective huddle

### AMBROSE, MO, AND ELLIOT

## Silurian Lab

The Silurians have built an advanced society thanks to their exploration of science. In a high-tech laboratory, Malohkeh conducts his experiments on the creatures he collects from the surface. His living database includes hedgehogs, domestic pets, a woolly mammoth, and even a human child. The control station for these activities is powered by geothermal energy, and can be programmed to release toxic fumes.

A laser scalpel can make highly accurate incisions. It is used for living autopsies—without anesthetic!

### LASER SCALPEL

Built-in power supply

Activation switch

### CENTRAL LAB CONTROL

Monitor displays vital life signs

Database contains 300 years worth of specimens

Organic fluid-control technology

Battle-scarred face

Warrior dress

Clothing denotes high military rank

Heat-ray gun

Human-like fingers

### RESTAC

Restac is Alaya's gene-twin, but as a military commander, she outranks her sister. She is charged with the security of the hibernating population. Some argue for peace and cohabitation with humans, but Restac has no time for that—she thinks executing the Doctor is a good way to send a message to the "apes."

Thirteen-year-old dyslexic Elliot is the latest addition to Malohkeh's list of experiments. His life cycle is slowed to one millionth of the normal rate, leaving him unresponsive and with a blank stare. Tubes of green fluid keep him alive with essential nutrients.

Shape designed to fit human specimens

Shackles hold wrists and ankles

### ALAYA

Dedicated to ridding Earth of humanity, Alaya is a soldier happy to die for her cause. In fact, she taunts Ambrose into killing her. She believes her murder will trigger a human-Silurian war, enabling her race to reclaim Earth's surface.

### STRETCHER

Those unfortunate enough to find themselves on Malohkeh's study list are strapped to a stretcher for "decontamination." This process neutralizes harmful bacteria and viruses.

# SILURIAN WARRIORS

THE FIERCELY PROTECTIVE Silurian race established a warrior caste to keep its cities safe from the dinosaurs that roamed Earth at that time. For these warriors, nothing is more important than the survival of their reptilian species. Now awake after eons hibernating underground, the warriors are furious that humanity has overrun "their" home. They see humans as vermin—just like the primitive apes they encountered millennia ago.

## Sisters in Arms

With special training and fearsome armor, Silurian warriors such as Restac and Alaya are creatures of precision, beauty, and absolute deadliness. With superior Silurian technology, these humanoid, cold-blooded reptiles believe they can reclaim the surface of Earth. For these soldiers, violence is always the answer.

Tough ridges of bone protect Silurian skull

Venom glands take 24 hours to refill

Hole in battle mask for forked tongue to lash out and strike opponents

Military uniform of the Silurian warrior caste

Tailor-made armor fits tight to body

Chain mail forged from underground metals

Form-fitting mesh protects legs but allows freedom of movement

Heavy boots needed for tough underground terrain

RESTAC

ALAYA

### HEAT RAY GUN

Molecular acceleration barrel

Safety button

Barrel emits a wide dispersing heat beam

This primitive-looking but technologically advanced gun fires deadly heat rays. Ornately decorated, it's a piece of art to be admired, as well a weapon to be feared.

Sun visors shield eyes used to living underground

Mouth fixed in a sinister expression

### BATTLE MASK

As a sign of honor and also for protection, Silurian warriors wear battle masks that are molded to fit closely to the very fronts of their faces. A flexible armored gorget protects their vulnerable neck area.

# MADAME VASTRA

A NOBLE SILURIAN WARRIOR, Madame Vastra was awoken from hibernation by London Underground workers, who accidentally caused the deaths of her sisters. Vastra was in the process of avenging them when the Doctor intervened, after which she chose a different path. Now, instead of working to destroy humanity, she lives in Victorian England, solving strange and disturbing crimes as leader of the Paternoster Gang.

Bandolier for extra weapons

Gently curved long sword for battle

Tough leather combat boots

## A Noble Warrior

An intelligent and capable warrior, Vastra is not only effective at armed combat, but her battle experiences have also developed her skills as a master strategist. She is highly intuitive, relying on instinct to predict her enemies' actions.

Known informally as the "Veiled Detective," Vastra specializes in seemingly unsolvable cases. One of her great successes is the capture of the infamous serial killer, Jack the Ripper, whose body Vastra then devoured.

Over the years, Vastra has developed great affection for the Doctor. In the Eleventh Doctor's hour of need, when his death seems close at hand, she gathers those close to him, determined to protect her old friend.

Dagger for short-range fighting

Victorian-inspired corset

Skintight leather combat clothing often worn beneath Victorian dress

During the epic battle of Demon's Run, Vastra and Jenny display their incredible sword-fighting prowess against the Headless Monks in a bid to protect Amy Pond and her baby, Melody.

A Silurian, a Sontaran, and a human make up the Paternoster Gang—an unlikely trio of amateur sleuths. Stubborn Vastra, weapons-obsessed Strax, and feisty, sarcastic Jenny investigate the murky underworld of Victorian England, dispensing their version of justice to both local criminals and aliens alike.

## Jenny Flint

Jenny is Madame Vastra's dedicated and trustworthy maid. Over time, the pair have become close and are now married, working together as they carry out their investigations. Like Vastra, Jenny is an expert fighter, as skilled in hand-to-hand combat as she is wielding a sword.

# THE PANDORICA

LEGEND HAS IT THAT the Pandorica is a box designed as a prison to hold the most feared thing in all the universe: a nameless, terrible monster soaked in the blood of a million galaxies. The Doctor is familiar with the tale, but he never imagined that the description could fit him, and that he is the intended inhabitant of the Pandorica. The Doctor, River Song, and Amy Pond find the Pandorica in an ancient weathered chamber beneath Stonehenge.

Center pin pops out to allow the sections to rotate

The patterns on the side of the Pandorica are made up of intricately carved stone pieces that interlock like a 3-D puzzle box. When the unlocking process is triggered from inside, these layers of locks move apart and rotate.

Hand can drop away to reveal Auton gun-stick

Realistic period clothing

## The Pandorica Opens

A gleaming black cube 10 feet (3 meters) square, the Pandorica is a formidable fortress with layers of security protocols: deadlocks, time-stops, matter lines. It has been waiting for the Doctor in an old dark chamber called the "underhenge" hidden below Stonehenge. It takes only one scan of the biometric data from the Doctor's handprint for it to unlock itself. The Doctor is curious to know what is inside, unaware that the Pandorica is opening to receive him.

Intricate inlaid patterns in ancient glyphs

Layers of locking mechanisms unlock from the inside

### AMY'S BOOKS

Information from books that Amy read as a child—about Pandora's Box and the Romans—inform the scenario the Nestene create to ensnare the Doctor.

## Fake Romans

Above the Pandorica, it appears to be Roman Britain, but everything is a fabrication created as a trap by the Nestene Consciousness, formed from an imprint of Amy's memories. The Roman Army is the greatest human military machine ever known, but these centurions are not human, let alone Roman.

## AUTON GUN-STICK

Gun can shoot or vaporize targets

Jointed fingers solidify when gun activated

Box emits an energy forcefield that can extend over the whole of Stonehenge

Chair forces prisoner to stay alive

## The Auton Deceit

The Roman soldiers are Autons—living plastic in a human shape controlled by the Nestene Consciousness. Soldiers appear human until they glaze over, turn in unison, and raise their hands to reveal considerably more firepower than a sword or bow and arrow.

The illusion created by the Nestene is highly convincing, with a full Roman encampment near Stonehenge. However, a scan reveals that energy weapons have been used here.

While the Pandorica is open, time energy is eating up the universe, wiping many races from existence. Some turn to stone, as after-images of creatures that now never existed.

## The Anomaly Exhibition

After 2,000 years, the Pandorica turns up at the Anomaly Exhibition, a display of impossible things at the National Museum in London. Surrounded by myth and legend, it was discovered under Stonehenge in 107AD and taken back to Rome. Stolen by Goths, and sold by Marco Polo, it was later recovered from the Aegean seabed. During the Blitz in World War II it was rescued from a burning warehouse in London.

# THE ALLIANCE

OVER THE CENTURIES, many aliens have crossed swords with the Doctor. Daleks, Cybermen, and many other races join in an unlikely alliance to build the Pandorica to put an end to the Doctor once and for all. When the Pandorica opens, they all receive notification from a transmission boosted by Stonehenge. They gather in the skies over Earth in their billions to see the Doctor locked in the prison.

**CYBERMAN**

The Cybermen display advanced space and time travel skills when they arrive on Earth to join the Alliance.

At first, the Doctor is bemused that the prison is for him. He is astonished that it took such an alliance to entrap him and that he is seen as a great warrior. But when the gravity of the situation becomes clear, he is angry and then remorseful. He feels the pain he has inflicted while saving one species from another.

## Allies with a Cause

In a far future event, the TARDIS explodes and the Eye of Harmony within it causes temporal energy to burn at every point in time and space simultaneously. Cracks begin to appear across the universe. Some are tiny and some are big enough for whole planets to fall through. The light pouring out the cracks carries so much temporal power that it wipes from existence anything it touches—so all species across the universe come together to lock up the Doctor and prevent this event from ever happening.

## The Cyber Sentry

The Cybermen posted to watch over the Pandorica have stood guard for so long that their organic parts have rotted. However, their metal components are still active and are just as deadly. Although dismembered, their wires spread around the underhenge, searching for fresh meat to replace their decayed organs.

**CYBERHEAD SENTRY**

The Pandorica chamber also contains petrified Cybermen parts. Time energy seeping from cracks in the Universe have caused the Cybermen to cease to exist, leaving just a stone imprint of their memory.

**STONE CYBERMAN SENTRY**

**SONTARAN**

Sontaran Commander Stark leads the Sontaran present at the Pandorica.

## JUDOON

The armed Judoon, led by their captain, personally help force the Doctor into his prison.

## ROBOFORM

Roboforms are scavengers that normally accompany other races on invasions.

## SUPREME DALEK

Daleks are not known for cooperating, but their hatred of the Doctor is greater than their hatred of other races.

## SILURIAN

A small group of Silurians reveal that they still count the Doctor as their enemy when they turn up at Stonehenge.

## AUTON

The Nestene Consciousness uses Auton slaves disguised as Roman soldiers to trick the Doctor and guard the Pandorica prison.

## UVODNI

The Uvodni are a humanoid race with insectoid faces from the Spiral Cluster of the Dragon Nebula.

## SYCORAX

Some Sycorax warriors also obey the summons to join the Alliance.

# PEG DOLLS

To BEGIN WITH, the Peg Dolls are ordinary wooden dolls inhabiting a dollhouse, which belongs to a young boy named George. However, George is not a regular human child, but part of an alien species called the Tenza. George uses his psycho-kinetic powers to send all his fears into the dollhouse—which causes the Peg Dolls to come to life and transform anyone they touch into living dolls as well.

George has taken on the appearance of a regular human child

## GEORGE THE TENZA

Like other Tenza, George hatched in space then sought out foster parents for himself. However, he believes the human parents he chose are rejecting him, and as a result, is subconsciously trapping all his worst fears in the dolls' house.

Old-fashioned toy soldier uniform

Long, straggly hair sprouts from victim's head

Painted face is chipped and cracked

Limbs lumber and walk in awkward fashion

Wooden arms open wide to ensnare more victims

## George's Dad

George's foster dad Alex is desperate to help his son overcome his fears and seeks medical help. However, he doesn't realize that George thinks the "Doctor" has come to take him away—escalating the young Tenza's terror, and causing the Doctor and Alex to enter the dollhouse.

As George himself enters the dollhouse and is about to be transformed by the Peg Dolls, Alex tells his son that he'll never send him away—allaying George's fears and restoring everything to normality.

## Living Dolls

When a person is turned into a Peg Doll, their body parts grow larger bit by bit, swiftly changing into wood. With all trace of personality lost, the end result is a terrifying toy that lumbers around the doll-house in a state of living death.

# HANDBOTS

THE CLINICALLY WHITE HANDBOTS are medical robots designed to look after people suffering from the fatal Chen 7 plague in the Two Streams Facility on the planet Apalapucia. Limited in intelligence and physical agility, the robots are equipped with hypodermic needles and darts for administering medicine. They lack eyes in the conventional sense, instead using their hand sensors to "see" where they're going.

Visor lifts up over head

Face older and wrinkled

Wooden staff

Makeshift armor

Heavy sword effective against Handbots

### THE GIRL WHO WAITED

Trapped in the accelerated time stream of plague-infested Apalapucia while the Handbots believe she needs anesthetizing, one version of Amy Pond waits 36 years for the Doctor and Rory to rescue her. She becomes embittered and careworn in the process.

Hand delivers anesthetic by touch

Head opens up to reveal medical dart

Chest compartment stores hypodermic syringes

Glass resembles oversized magnifying glass

### TIME GLASS

In the Two Streams Facility, infected patients with only 24 hours to live are placed in a faster time stream, allowing them to "live" their full lives in a single day. A Time Glass syncs the faster time stream with the normal world, allowing visitors to communicate with the patients. Rory and the Doctor use it to reach Amy.

Two-way communication interface

### Rorybot

Starved of human friendship, the trapped, aging Amy creates her own companion by disarming a Handbot and drawing a smiley face on it. She names it Rory after the boyfriend she thinks she'll never see again.

## Organic Robots

The Handbots have sensitive organic skin grafted onto their hands for sensing bacteria in their surroundings. As well as delivering anesthetic, the robotic hands can complete detailed scans of their environment and even register the presence of bacteria on a patient.

The Handbots are limited and unable to sense that Amy's human body would be unable to cope with their medicine. To prevent them from giving her what could be a lethal injection, she becomes something of an expert at disabling and reprogramming the machines.

# THE *FANCY*

A GHOSTLY GREEN APPARITION is terrorizing the crew of the becalmed pirate ship the *Fancy*. Its captain, Henry Avery, believes they are being attacked by the mythical Siren, a beautiful being which rises from the ocean each time one of his men is injured. Lulled by the Siren's haunting singing, Avery's crew members are being atomized one by one.

## The Black Spot

Every time someone is wounded, a black spot suddenly appears on the palm of his hand. The pirates believe this means just one thing: that the Siren has marked her latest victim for death.

Black spot on the hand of pirate McGrath

Mop used as makeshift weapon against Siren

17th century pirate dress

Tricorn sailor's hat

Keys to ship's armory and store-rooms

Flintlock pistol

FLORRES

DANCER

CAPTAIN AVERY

BOATSWAIN

## The Siren

The Siren is really a virtual doctor from a spaceship trapped in a parallel reality. Since the ship's alien crew was destroyed by a human virus, the ghostly doctor has been teleporting Avery's crew aboard in order to heal them.

## Captain Avery

Formerly a respected naval officer, Avery turned to piracy and abandoned his wife and young son, Toby. When he realizes that Toby has stowed away onboard, he is unable to admit what he has become and believes he's an unfit father for the boy.

When Rory accidentally cuts himself, he suddenly finds the Siren's eerie song utterly irresistible. His friends have to hold him back to stop him from trying to touch the creature.

Avery's son has typhoid fever, and so, Avery decides to stay and care for him under the Siren's medical protection. Along with his pirate crew, he sails the *Fancy* out into space.

# MINOTAUR

A TERRIFYING, HORNED CREATURE, the Minotaur stalks the corridors of a strange hotel full of people's worst nightmares. At first, it seems the Minotaur is feeding on the fear of those trapped in the hotel, but when it starts killing people, the Doctor realizes that the beast is actually feasting on their faith—literally draining the life from its victims.

Multiple horns at front and rear of head

Open mouth for communicating with guttural growls

Powerful arms and fists

Fists clenched in frustration and anger

Ragged, primitive-style clothing

Cloven hooves

The hotel is actually an automated spaceship prison, built by a race that had once worshipped the Minotaur before turning against it and casting it off into space. The prison is programmed to trap other life forms and convert their faith into food for the creature.

Each "hotel room" in the prison ship contains a disturbing vision for every being that's become trapped there. Amy Pond's room is probably the most terrifying of all—it contains Weeping Angels.

Unable to stop the Minotaur hunting people down and killing them, the Doctor decides to go on the offensive instead. With everyone's help, he devises a plan to corner the beast and interrogate it.

## Overthrown Deity

After being imprisoned for thousands of years, all the Minotaur longs for is death. However, the beast's survival instinct is too strong and it can't help but feast on each new source of faith energy. Eventually, the Doctor succeeds in severing its supply, giving the Minotaur the space it needs to die at long last.

The Minotaur is captured in the hotel's beauty parlor, but like a cornered bull, it proves impossible to contain for very long. Driven by rage and instinct, it begins to smash the place up before making its escape.

In order to mentally control their Gangers, the Morpeth Jetsan miners remain in a dormant state. If this link is broken, it is possible for the Gangers to become independent beings.

# GANGERS

IN THE 22ND CENTURY, duplicates of humans known as Gangers (shortened from "Doppelgängers") are used in environments that are too dangerous for real people to work in. Formed from an artificial substance called the Flesh, the beings are telepathically controlled by their human counterparts. Whenever a Ganger gets damaged or destroyed, another duplicate can be created with ease.

Flashlight for low-light mining conditions

Logo of acid-mining company, Morpeth Jetsan

White face shows that Ganger has not fully stabilized

Metallic implements used as weapons

Gangers wear the same clothes as their original human counterparts

DICKEN

MIRANDA CLEAVES

JIMMY WICKS

BUZZER

## Rebel Flesh

When a solar tsunami hits an acid mine on a remote island, the link between the human miners and their duplicates is severed and the Gangers become independent, with their own thoughts and feelings. Humans and Gangers are mistrustful of the other, and the threatened Gangers plot to kill the humans in order to ensure their own survival.

## Ganger Creation

Creating a Ganger is a complex technological process. First, a special harness scans the molecular structure of a human. Next, a vat of Flesh slowly fills up a human-sized tank until it is brimming with the gooey white substance. Slowly, facial features begin to form, the process continues until a perfect Ganger copy has been created.

Thick metal walls to prevent leakage

Power source connected to electrical mains

Length of tank allows it to contain whole human being

TANK FOR THE FLESH

When the Doctor scans the Flesh, it somehow makes a mental connection with him. He realizes that the substance is sentient in a way no one else can comprehend.

## Doctor Ganger

A Ganger version of the Doctor is accidentally created after the real Doctor leaves a genetic imprint on the Flesh. Behaving much like his alter ego, the Ganger fools even Amy Pond into believing he is the real Doctor.

JENNIFER LUCAS

Cloned face

A solar storm wreaks havoc on the acid mine. Not only does it cause the power surge that creates the rebel Gangers, but it also causes the mine's pipes to crack, leaking lethal acid everywhere.

Recovering from the infighting at the mine, three Gangers, including Miranda Cleaves and Dicken, survive. Thanks to the TARDIS's energy, they fully stabilize as people. They now face the daunting task of making everyone understand the plight of Gangers across the world.

Unstable Flesh molecules allow for unnatural flexibility

## Ganger Jennifer

The multiple Ganger versions of Morpeth Jetsan worker Jennifer Lucas are less stable than those of her colleagues'. Not remembering that the humans on the island were once her fellow workers, she plots to kill them by causing the mine's acid to explode—after which, she intends to inspire a Ganger revolution worldwide. She eventually transforms into a deranged Flesh monster, and is destroyed by the Ganger Doctor.

## Amy Substitute

As awareness of Gangers is spread across the universe, it opens up the possibility that people might use them for evil. The Order of Silence, led by Madame Kovarian, kidnaps a pregnant Amy Pond and replaces her with a Ganger copy, which the Doctor eventually destroys. They plan to keep her safe until her baby is born, at which point they substitute the baby too, hoping to brainwash her into becoming the Doctor's killer.

# THE ORDER OF SILENCE

THE SILENCE IS A RELIGIOUS ORDER dedicated to preventing the Doctor from reaching the planet Trenzalore. They believe that his presence there would allow the Time Lords to return to the universe, causing the Time War to begin all over again. The Silence therefore decide to travel back along the Doctor's time stream, going to desperate lengths in their attempts to kill him.

Eye-drive enables wearer to remember the memory-proof Silents

## Madame Kovarian

A key figure in the Kovarian Chapter of the Silence, Madame Kovarian is ruthlessly dedicated to bringing about the Doctor's destruction. Her main task is to kidnap Amy Pond's baby, Melody, and brainwash her into becoming the Doctor's killer—a psychopath otherwise known as River Song.

Expecting trouble from the Doctor, the Silence have amassed a vast army of Clerics—highly trained soldiers who are dedicated to ensuring that their overriding mission is successful.

When Madame Kovarian is captured in an alternative timeline, she is horrified to discover that she has become dispensable to the Silence and is killed by her own electrified eye-drive.

During one assassination attempt on the Doctor, Kovarian and the Silence kidnap the grown-up River Song and place her in an armed, automated spacesuit beneath Lake Silencio in Utah. They believe they have engineered a fixed point in time. However, when River rises from the lake, she refuses to gun down the Doctor and time itself unravels.

One of many smart, crisp business suits, normally worn in black

Fiercely sharp high heels

## ORDER OF SILENCE FACTS

■ The Order of Silence was created by Tasha Lem, Mother Superior of the Papal Mainframe.

■ Members of the Order have the power to time travel.

■ In one attempt to kill the Doctor, they blew up the TARDIS, unwittingly causing the universe to collapse.

■ Also calling themselves the "Sentinels of History," the Order's core belief is that "Silence must fall." It means that the Doctor must never be allowed to speak his name and free the Time Lords, thus potentially restarting the Time War.

# The Silents

Tall, skeletal humanoids, the Silents are confessional priests, genetically engineered by the Papal Mainframe to be memory-proof so that people would forget everything they'd told them. A group of the creatures travels back in time with Madame Kovarian to help her attempt to kill the Doctor. They are a dangerous enemy to have: they can absorb electricity from their surroundings into their bodies, before discharging it again through their fingers. The resultant blast is powerful enough to reduce a human to charred cinders.

Mouth opens wide during electrical absorption

Sunken eyes within hollow, terrifying faces

After looking away from a Silent, people forget that the creature ever existed. One way to record an encounter with a Silent is to draw tally marks while still looking at it—to act as a reminder of how many times the aliens have been encountered.

The Silents have influenced the world throughout history, using their powers of post-hypnotic suggestion to make humanity do their will. They even inspired mankind's desire to go to the Moon so that it would develop spacesuit technology. Even US President Nixon becomes involved in the quest to stop them.

Kovarian Chapter Silents wear shirt and tie

The Silents are devious creatures. In an alternative timeline, they allow themselves to be imprisoned inside glass tanks, but far from being dormant, they are really lying in wait for the Doctor.

The Doctor encounters the Silents creatures again on the planet Trenzalore. In that final battle, they actually join forces with the Doctor against the Daleks, proving that old enemies can fight side by side.

Elongated fingers, from which lightning bolts can be discharged

# DEMON'S RUN

A REMOTE ASTEROID, Demon's Run is the Order of Silence's secret military base and the scene of a great battle in which the Doctor attempts to rescue his companion Amy Pond and her baby, Melody. The asteroid's name hails from a prophetic poem containing the line "Demons run when a good man goes to war." Assuming himself to be that man, and calling in some old debts, the Doctor gathers together an unlikely band of fighters to help overcome the massed forces of the Silence.

## The Headless Monks

One of the Silence's principal allies, the Headless Monks are a deeply religious order who choose to decapitate themselves as they believe in following their hearts rather than their minds. On Demon's Run, the Monks do not register as alive on scanning equipment—an advantage that allows them to mount surprise attacks.

Before a fight, the Headless Monks chant a sacred attack prayer. During battle they fire lethal blasts of energy from their hands and fight with electrified swords.

Loose skin left from removal of head twisted into a knot

Hood normally raised to cover headless state

Hands outstretched for shooting balls of energy

Simple monks' robes

## Colonel Manton

Insignia denoting rank of Colonel

Colonel Manton is in charge of military operations on Demon's Run, determined to boost his troops' morale in preparation for an attack by the Doctor. However, when the Doctor tricks Manton's forces into disarming themselves, he tells the Colonel to order his men to run away, hoping that the disgraced leader will be forever known as "Colonel Runaway."

## LORNA BUCKET

Lorna met the Doctor briefly when she was a little girl. She believed him to be a great warrior and so joined the Church's army of clerics in the hope of encountering her hero again. On Demon's Run, she switches sides and joins the Doctor's army of allies, but is tragically killed by the Headless Monks.

Some of the Doctor's closest allies are Madame Vastra, her partner, Jenny, and Strax the Sontaran nurse. They bravely defend Amy and her baby against the Headless Monks' brutal attack, which results in Strax's apparent death.

Dressed in his Roman centurion clothes, Rory displays superb sword-fighting skills and survives the battle against the Monks. Soon he is also fighting to save his newborn baby, Melody, from the Order of the Silence.

The Doctor's influence stretches far and wide. He calls on the Silurians and Judoon to help his friends take on the Silence. He even gets his old pal Winston Churchill to send a squadron of space-faring Spitfires to take out Demon's Run's communications array.

Media chip implanted in head can receive wi-fi

Bright blue skin

Opulent robes and expensive jewelry

## Dorium Maldovar

A fat, blue-skinned alien, Dorium is a wealthy wheeler dealer who always has his ear to the ground. He sells the Headless Monks the security software they need to imprison Amy's child, but later switches sides when the Doctor calls on him to repay an old debt. During battle, he attempts to sweet-talk the Headless Monks into sparing him, but instead they chop off his head.

A shifty alien named Gantok is a servant to the Silence, but he agrees to take the Doctor to Dorium Maldovar's head in the underground tunnel of skulls. Only the wealthiest can afford boxes for their severed heads. The walls of the tunnels are lined with loose, mean-spirited, skulls capable of devouring a man.

The Headless Monks place Dorium's head in box and store it in the Seventh Transept. Dorium remains alive in this state and is able to tell the Doctor about the Silence and their reasons for wanting to prevent him from reaching Trenzalore.

# TRENZALORE

A LEVEL TWO HUMAN COLONY, Trenzalore is a world of enormous significance to the Doctor. It is a planet he finds himself defending in order to prevent the Time War beginning anew between the Time Lords and the rest of the universe. In an alternative timeline, it is also the place where the Doctor discovers that his body is buried.

Physiogonomy is probably mostly human

Body does not age

Clothes are a holographic projection

## A Crack in the Universe

In the town of Christmas on Trenzalore, the Doctor finds a familiar-looking crack in a wall—the last remaining tear in the skin of reality. Trapped in a pocket universe, the Time Lords are beaming a truth field and an endlessly repeating question, "Doctor who?", through the gap. The Doctor realizes that if he answers with his real name, the Time Lords will know it's safe to come through and return, possibly triggering a new Time War.

## The Papal Mainframe

As the security hub of the known universe, the Papal Mainframe seeks to prevent war from breaking out. This "church" is both mysterious, and, at times, controversial. It consists of different, often heavily armed, factions, including more violent groups that have broken away—such as the Doctor's old foe Madame Kovarian.

When the Daleks invade the Papal Mainframe as a means to reach Trenzalore, they slaughter Tasha Lem before harvesting information from her body. She is turned into a Dalek puppet, but the Doctor manages to restore strong-minded Tasha's true personality once again, turning her against her Dalek masters.

## Tasha Lem

Otherwise known as the Mother Superior, Tasha Lem is an old friend of the Doctor's and the powerful head of the Church of the Papal Mainframe. She protects Trenzalore with a forcefield, realizing that if the Doctor gives his name, the Time Lords will return and the Time War will begin anew. She therefore dedicates her church to a new cause, declaring that "Silence will fall," meaning the Doctor must be prevented from speaking his name at all costs.

## A Town called Christmas

Snow-farming villages like Christmas can be found across Trenzalore. The presence of the crack in time and space, however, marks Christmas out to receive attention and bombardment from alien forces. The Doctor decides to become the sheriff of this village in order to protect both his own race, the Time Lords, and his new home on Trenzalore, fighting off alien attempts to invade with the help of the Papal Mainframe.

Woolen cap wards off cold

Colorful clothes of Christmas residents

Shorts worn by junior citizens

### BARNABLE

A young boy named Barnable is one of the many human villagers that the Doctor befriends over the centuries. He and the Doctor become very attached to one another after the Doctor saves Barnable's father's barn from destruction.

The friendly villagers of Christmas welcome the Doctor, and will always answer any question honestly, due to the truth field imposed by the Time Lords.

Countless alien races travel in their spaceships to Trenzalore to investigate the potential Time Lord threat, including the Daleks, Sontarans, and the Cybermen.

Wood untouchable by the Doctor's sonic screwdriver

Flamethrower weapon built into arm

### WOODEN CYBERMAN

The Papal Mainframe places technology sensors around Christmas to alert the Doctor to the presence of approaching alien enemies. Undeterred, the invading Cybermen downgrade to be made of wood—which doesn't set off the sensors.

The Doctor is prepared to grow old and die defending Trenzalore, even when the Daleks send for reinforcements and break through the Papal Mainframe's defenses. In events that rewrite time, the Time Lords gift the Doctor new regenerations, ensuring his survival, the safety of the people of Trenzalore, and the Daleks' defeat.

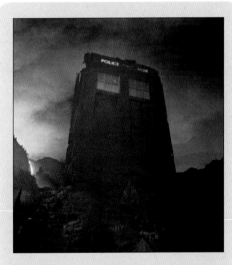

### The Doctor's Grave

In an alternative timeline, Trenzalore is a desolate battlefield graveyard and the location for the Doctor's tomb. In this version of events, the Doctor pays his first visit to the planet after his friends in the Paternoster Gang are kidnapped by the Great Intelligence. His grave is marked by a damaged future version of his TARDIS, which has grown to an enormous size. Fortunately, this timeline is aborted when the Time Lords change the future and grant him a new set of regenerations.

# KAHLER

A TECHNOLOGICALLY GIFTED race, the Kahler suffered a terrible war which wiped out half of their planet. Tasked with restoring peace, a team of scientists including Kahler-Jex experimented on innocent volunteers, turning them into cyborg killers who defeated the enemy. However, one of the cyborgs, Kahler-Tek, wants revenge on its creators and tracks Jex to the American town of Mercy.

Distinctive Kahler markings

Cybernetic eye with in-built sensors

Spare energy cells for laser weapon

Arm replaced with high-intensity laser weapon

Clothing damaged during combat

The people of Mercy, a small town in 1870s America, face a dilemma—either they hand over Kahler-Jex to the Gunslinger, or they face starvation.

Isaac is Mercy's brave and wise sheriff. When he is accidentally gunned down by Kahler-Tek, the sheriff hands his badge to the Doctor, telling him to protect both Jex and his town.

## Kahler-Jex

Although he saved millions of lives, scientist Jex regrets performing the cruel experiments that turned people into monsters. To atone for his crimes, he saves the townsfolk of Mercy from cholera, and gives them electricity.

Kahler-Jex uses his crashed spaceship as a generator to bring electricity to Mercy. The Doctor probes its data banks to reveal the truth about Jex's past.

Thanks to its cybernetic eye, Kahler-Tek has an automatic targetting mode, making the cyborg a highly efficient killer.

Appalled by Kahler-Jex's atrocities, an angry Doctor attempts to hand him over to the Gunslinger. Thanks to Amy's intervention, he reconsiders. However, the war-weary scientist is unable to reconcile himself to his past actions, and blows up his spaceship while sitting inside it.

## Kahler-Tek

Otherwise known as the Gunslinger, Kahler-Tek is half-man, half-machine. Determined to kill Kahler-Jex for his monstrous experiments, he places Mercy under siege and demands that they hand over the war criminal—or face certain death themselves.

# SHAKRI

THE SHAKRI ARE mysterious beings who the Doctor mistakenly believed were only a myth to keep the young of Gallifrey in their place. Known as the pest controllers of the universe, the Shakri see humans as dangerous vermin who must be wiped out before they can colonize space.

Aged appearance

Somber black robes

Long, sharp fingernails

## Deadly Cubes

Serving an entity known as "the Tally," the Shakri deposit millions of small black boxes all over Earth to gather information about its inhabitants. When activated, each one sends out an electrical surge to stop the heart of the nearest human.

The Shakri have seven spacecraft in another dimension, connected to Earth via seven portals. The Doctor locates a portal in a nearby hospital where he also finds an outlier droid in the form of a young girl, used by the invaders to monitor the vicinity.

## Orderlies

Silent, creepy humanoids with grills for mouths, the Orderlies' function is to kidnap hospital patients and take them aboard the Shakri spaceship. They defend themselves with large hypodermic syringes.

The automated Shakri interface is helpless when the Doctor disrupts the Shakri computer systems and manages to disconnect the Shakri craft from their portals, leaving them drifting in dark space. Even better, the Doctor uses the cubes to turn their victims hearts on once again.

## Automated Interface

The Doctor is denied knowledge of what the Shakri really look like. When he finally makes contact with the Shakri ship responsible for dumping the black cubes on Earth he is greeted by a hologram taking the form of a black-cloaked humanoid. This sinister apparition warns that the Shakri plan to release a second wave of cubes and cause further deaths.

# AKHATEN

A PARASITIC, SENTIENT PLANET, Akhaten is treated fearfully as a vengeful god by the Sun-singers of Akhet—the inhabitants of the seven neighboring worlds. Known as the "Old God," Akhaten has been kept asleep for millions of years, thanks to "The Long Song"—a never-ending lullaby sung by successive generations of Sun-singer choristers.

A host of aliens have gathered on the orbiting asteroid Tiannamat, including Panbabylonians, Hooloovoos, Ultramantas, and Terraberserkers. They have all come for the Festival of Offerings, where each creature presents a treasured gift to the "Old God" Akhaten.

High-domed skull

Ancient, emaciated appearance

Garland presented during the Festival of Offerings

## Queen of Years

The title of the "Queen of Years" has been bestowed on a young girl named Merry. In this role, she is expected to sing to the Old God, and know every song, poem, and legend from the Sun-singers' history. Merry, however, is ignorant of the Queen of Years' other duty— to be sacrificed. The locals believe it is their job to sacrifice the queen to Akhaten. Otherwise, Akhaten will feed on the souls of everyone on the seven planets, and then in the universe beyond.

Unaware of the Queen of Years' sacrificial role, Merry resists being taken. She thinks that she is being punished for performing her song wrong. Her struggle causes the Long Song to end and Akhaten to awaken.

MERRY GEJELH

The Vigil are mysterious beings with telekinetic powers who stand guard in the Mummy's temple. Once Akhaten awakens, it has no further use for its servants. The Vigil vanish into thin air, and the Mummy starts dying inside its shattered cell.

Long talons and powerful arms for breaking down cell

The Doctor confronts Akhaten, hoping to overload the parasite with his countless memories. Clara then joins the fight, offering it a precious leaf which represents all the days her mom could have had, if she hadn't died young. Overwhelmed, Akhaten implodes.

## The Mummy

Trapped in a glass cell within a pyramid-shaped temple on an orbiting asteroid, the Mummy serves as Akhaten's alarm clock. A primitive, savage creature, it communicates with guttural snarls and growls. Placed to warn the Old God when the Long Song ends, the beast sends a signal, causing it to awaken.

# SWEETVILLE

IN 1893, MRS. GILLYFLOWER is recruiting people to live in the idyllic Yorkshire, England community of Sweetville, although she seems interested only in the fittest, brightest, and most beautiful applicants. Advertised as a safe haven where people have a chance to survive a coming apocalypse, Sweetville turns out to be a front for Mrs. Gillyflower's plan to create a "perfect" world.

Mr. Sweet is a tiny red leech from the time of the dinosaurs and Silurians, which has somehow managed to survive. A parasitic creature, it has attached itself to Mrs. Gillyflower's chest. In return for sustenance, it provides her with the deadly venom she needs and has become physically dependent upon. She refers to him as her "silent partner".

Slow-moving body

## MR. SWEET

Modest dress of a Victorian puritan

Outer garments conceal Mr. Sweet

Black widow's gown

It may look like the perfect place to live, but nobody residing in Sweetville is ever seen again.

To aid her recruitment drive, Mrs. Gillyflower issues sermons full of warnings of the End of Days, neglecting to mention it is she who intends to destroy mankind.

Scarred face and blindness caused by leech venom

## ADA GILLYFLOWER

The gentle and devoted daughter of Mrs. Gillyflower, Ada is the victim of her mother's experiments with red leech venom in her attempts to discover an antitoxin. Ada is devastated when she learns she is not part of her mother's plan for the new "perfect" world.

## Winifred Gillyflower

A prize-winning chemist and mechanical engineer, Mrs. Gillyflower is a puritan with an insane vision for humanity. She plans to load the venom produced by Mr. Sweet onto a rocket, explode it in the atmosphere, and bring about an apocalypse. She will then create a new world, populated only by her chosen, beautiful recruits.

Mrs. Gillyflower's chosen people, including Clara, are preserved beneath giant bell jars. The jar will protect them from the venom that will be showered over Earth.

Sweetville's rejects are cast into a nearby canal, their dead bodies glowing a suspicious bright red. The Doctor is amongst these, but his Time Lord body survives the toxic process that was meant to kill him.

Mrs. Gillyflower builds the rocket to fire the leech venom herself. As her plan progresses, she activates the rocket's firing mechanism—but is thwarted thanks to Madame Vastra and Jenny, who have removed its lethal cargo.

# ICE WARRIORS

NATIVES OF THE PLANET MARS, Ice Warriors are reptilian beings with a strong instinct for war. More than seven feet tall, the Martians developed mechanized armor to allow them to survive when their home planet turned cold. Inside a bulky protective shell is a wiry and cunning creature that is able to leave its armor and wreak havoc with astonishing agility.

Hammer and sickle emblem of the Soviet Union

Black Soviet naval uniform

Three stripes and star on sleeve insignia indicate Stepashin's rank

## LIEUTENANT STEPASHIN

A fiercely patriotic Soviet naval officer, Stepashin attacks the Ice Warrior Skaldak by electrocuting him. Stepashin remains loyal to his country by attempting to form an alliance with the Ice Warrior. But the Soviet officer underestimates Skaldak, and is killed by him.

Ice Warriors are naturally bloodthirsty. In a dangerous or unknown situation, their immediate response is to fight. When Grand Marshal Skaldak finds himself bound in chains onboard a Soviet submarine, he sends out a distress call to his fellow Ice Warriors. When he receives no reply, his thoughts turn to vengeance.

Like his fellow Ice Warriors, Skaldak has a strong sense of honor. He instinctively understands the concepts of war—and the merits of mercy. Skaldak arms the Soviet submarine's nuclear warheads, but is halted by the Doctor, who begs the Ice Warrior to act like a soldier, not a murderer.

Beneath their bio-armour, the Ice Warriors have a reptilian humanoid form. Skaldak has red glowing eyes, scaly skin, and rows of tiny, razor-sharp fangs.

Helmet flips upward to reveal face of occupant

Sonic weapon built into arm

The Ice Warriors travel through space in huge ships. When they receive a distress call from Earth, they come as fast as they can. The center of the ship has an opening through which Skaldak is teleported aboard, before returning to Mars.

## Grand Marshal Skaldak

The greatest Ice Warrior hero of all, Skaldak has been sleeping in the ice on Earth for over 5,000 years. When he's awoken and attacked by the crew of a Russian sub, the proud warrior honors his ancient Martian code by declaring war on humanity.

Survival armor capable of independent movement by remote control

# ZYGONS

SHAPE-SHIFTING ZYGONS have been waiting hundreds of years to invade Earth—ever since their own planet, Zygor, was destroyed during the Time War. With high-domed heads and sucker-covered skin, the creatures use their advanced body-print technology to copy and impersonate humans, making it easy for them to gain power by means of infiltration.

Venom sacs located in tongue

Suckered body

Stingers in hands can stun, maim and even kill

Thick, muscular legs lend huge strength to torso

Adept at manipulating the technology of other races, the Zygons succeed in hiding inside stasis cubes—Time Lord paintings, which are really frozen instants of time. The Zygons lie in wait for hundreds of years, then invade when Earth is sufficiently advanced and suitable for conquest.

When a Zygon changes back into its natural form, it spews out a red mucous from its mouth.

Regal Elizabethan dress emblazoned with jewels

## QUEEN ELIZABETH I

As the most powerful person in England, Queen Elizabeth attracts the attentions of the Zygons, becoming the primary target of their invasion attempt. A Zygon duplicate of the Queen attempts to kill her and take control of the country. However, the real Elizabeth kills her impersonator and infiltrates the Zygons' base. The Zygons realize that the time is not yet right to conquer Earth.

Zygon mimicry is so convincing, the Tenth Doctor finds it impossible to tell Queen Elizabeth apart from her Zygon double— even after kissing both of them!

The Zygons believe that alien artifacts contained within the secret vault at UNIT will help them conquer Earth. They impersonate UNIT's chief scientific officer, Kate Stewart, and succeed in infiltrating the so-called Black Archive.

## Invasion Party

The homeless Zygons plan to enslave humanity and alter Earth's climate in a bid to recreate the conditions of their home planet. Their attempt to invade through paintings is not their first—the aliens were once aided by a creature called the Skarasen, which was mistaken for the Loch Ness Monster!

Human brain held within metal exoskeleton

Some metalwork dates back to Roman times

Flame-emitting weapon concealed inside sleeve

Detachable hand capable of independent movement

Movement accompanied by sound of cogs in motion

# THE HALF-FACE MAN

LIKE A ROBOTIC VERSION of the infamous Frankenstein's monster, the Half-Face Man is a nightmarish cyborg that stalks the streets of Victorian London, hunting for human body parts. In reality, he is a repair droid from the SS *Marie Antoinette*, a spaceship from the 51st century that crash-landed on Earth millions of years ago. Along with the rest of his kind, the Half-Face Man has been constantly rebuilding himself with cannibalized organs ever since.

## Control Droid

The Half-Face Man is the control node for his fellow repair droids—when he comes to life, the others do too. Despite the fact that his ship has been buried underground for countless centuries, he has been determined to carry on functioning, requiring a fresh and constant supply of organs in order to remain operational. When asked about his true purpose, however, the robot gives the same strange answer— to reach the "Promised Land."

The repair droids will stop at nothing to ensure their continued survival. Much to the Doctor's horror, they even destroy a huge T-Rex in order to extract its optic nerve, which they then use to repair their computer systems.

### REPAIR DROID FACTS

- The SS *Marie Antoinette* is the sister ship of the SS *Madame de Pompadour*, which was run by similar repair droids.

- The Half-Face Man has replaced every mechanical and organic component of himself so many times, there is no longer any trace of the original left.

- When the Half-Face Man is destroyed, the other repair droids stop functioning as well.

Mask made of real human skin

Plain black and white outfit, suitable for use in Mancini's restaurant

The Half-Face Man is the manager of Mancini's restaurant, although the building is merely a front for the repair droids' gruesome operations. The upstairs area is populated with decoys—grotesque robotic diners who never eat anything but are equipped with multifunctional control devices disguised as pens. Used to scan other life forms, innocent people are then taken prisoner and sent down to the spaceship below, where their body parts are extracted.

The robotic droids recognize humans—a source of potential new body parts—by sensing their breath. Clara and the Doctor find themselves in mortal peril when catapulted from Mancini's restaurant into the heart of the robots' underground spaceship. Clara succeeds in holding her breath for a painfully long time in order to fool them—a ruse that works for a while, until she's found out and brought before the Half-Face Man for a terrifying interrogation.

The droids' restaurant is held within an escape pod—the only part of the spaceship that is still able to fly. When the roof opens up, a huge balloon made out of patches of stretched human skin begins to inflate, carrying the capsule up into the sky.

## THE DOCTOR IN DISGUISE

The Doctor disguises himself as a repair droid by putting on one of their creepy human masks. Not only does the ghoulish disguise deceive the robots, but it also fools Clara.

## Droid Army

The robots' underground ship is populated with dozens of sinister robots, each one dressed in ragged Victorian clothing.

### DROID DRESSED AS VICTORIAN SOLDIER

Unlike the droids in the restaurant, these are battle-ready, each with a lethal sword concealed in its sleeve, ready to slide out automatically.

Human face is easily detached

Visible seams where face is attached to head

Power source in the form of burning flame concealed inside skull

Blank, zombie-like expression

Extracted human organs in constant process of decay

FEMALE DISGUISE

MALE DISGUISE

# ROBOTS OF SHERWOOD

A FTER A SPACECRAFT crash-lands in Nottingham, England in the Middle Ages, both the ship and its robotic crew set about adapting to their new environment. The ship itself transforms into a twelfth-century castle, and while the robust robots seek to repair their craft, they take on the guise of knights in armor and seek out a new master to serve—the infamous Sheriff of Nottingham.

## Sheriff of Nottingham

An arrogant tyrant, the Sheriff is just as cruel and bloodthirsty as legend has portrayed him. Seriously injured when the spaceship fell to Earth, the robots reconstructed him using metallic components, to the extent that he is now a cyborg—half man, half robot. Not content with terrorizing the unfortunate inhabitants of Nottingham, the Sheriff has greater ambitions. He wants his robots to repair their spaceship so that he can fly to London and kill his unappreciative master, Prince John, claim the throne for himself and rule the entire world.

Cyborg head

Body capable of movement even when headless

Gold regarded as valuable by the robots, as it can be used to fix their ship

Tunic conceals device for controlling robots

Sword armed and dangerous

### Robot Knights

Thanks to their advanced technology, the robots have successfully adapted to blend seamlessly into their medieval surroundings. They appear to be ordinary knights in metal armor, but when they switch to battle mode, their true alien features are revealed and they begin to unleash their lethal firepower.

When lowered, helmet conceals metallic facial features

Boar traditionally symbolizes bravery and a willingness to fight to the very end

Hidden blasters fire purple-colored laser bolts

Armor protects robotic circuitry

KNIGHT WITH MECHANICAL FACE REVEALED

Soon after arriving in Sherwood Forest, the Doctor meets the legendary outlaw Robin Hood and his band of merry men—Will Scarlet, Friar Tuck, Alan-a-Dale, and Little John, all equally cheerful. The Doctor has a hard time believing that they actually exist, theorising he must have materialized inside either a miniscope, or possibly some kind of futuristic theme park.

## MECHANICAL MEN FACTS

■ Just like the robotic Half-Face Man, the Sheriff's robots were also on their way to the mysterious "Promised Land" when they crash-landed on Earth.

■ The robots' energy beams can be deflected with shiny objects such as shields or mirrors. Aiming this beam at the robots can destroy them.

■ The Sheriff has a hand-held device giving him complete control over his robot followers.

The damaged engines on the robots' spaceship are causing an odd effect. Radiation is leaking into the surrounding countryside—creating a temporary micro-climate where everything looks extra green and perfect. To repair the craft, the Sheriff sends his robots to steal gold from the locals, then melts it down to seal the engine breach. He doesn't realize, however, that the vessel is so badly damaged that it will explode on lift-off—taking half of England with it.

As good a swordsman as Robin is, he is no match for the Doctor and a small piece of cutlery. When Robin tries to steal the TARDIS from him, the Doctor fights back with his metal spoon, tripping Robin up and sending him sprawling into a nearby stream.

## GOLDEN ARROW

The prize of the Sheriff of Nottingham's archery contest, the golden arrow is rightfully won by skilled archer Robin. It serves another purpose when the outlaw fires it at the robots' spaceship as it takes off. The arrow weighs just the right amount to help the crippled ship reach orbit, where it explodes harmlessly.

Straight shaft allows archer to achieve deadly accuracy

Pure gold from head to fletchings

Bow for use in archery competitions

Felt cap worn to disguise face when in public

Long hair regarded as ridiculous by Doctor

Lightweight armor does not inhibit in combat

Green is perfect camouflage for hiding in Sherwood Forest

## The Legendary Robin Hood

The permanently grinning Robin Hood is instantly disliked by the Doctor. Not only is he annoyed by Robin's constant laughing, but he also believes that the outlaw is too physically perfect to be real and deduces that he must be another of the Sheriff's robots. Much to the Doctor's astonishment, however, Robin turns out to be a real-life flesh and blood human. He really is Robert, Earl of Loxley—a man who is determined to be a hero for those who have suffered under the Sheriff's tyrannical rule.

# KARABRAXOS

**O**N A BLEAK, DESERT WORLD is a single city, dominated by the pyramid-shaped building of the Bank of Karabraxos. It is supposedly the most dangerous bank in the galaxy and completely impregnable, thanks to the sophisticated security protocols that protect its precious contents. High above the arid surface, a solar storm is brewing in the planet's atmosphere, threatening to disrupt the banks' security systems. Below ground, the bank's vaults and passageways stretch down to the very core of the planet and harbor many sinister secrets.

Professional, perfectly styled coiffure

Outfit conceals activating button that allows access to the bank's public address system

The main bank vault is protected by multiple time-delayed locking codes, which must be cracked individually to obtain access. One of the vault's security protocols is a supposedly unbreakable atomic seal which is eventually tripped when the solar storm strikes an antenna on top of the building. Inside the vault are thousands of metal safes, which the Doctor discovers have also been opened by the solar disruption.

## Ms. Delphox

Cold and aloof, Ms Delphox is Head of Security at the Bank of Karabraxos. Together with her terrifying Teller creature, she deals with potential criminal activity with ruthless efficiency, determined to reinforce her bank's reputation of impregnability. Despite her powerful position, Ms Delphox lives in constant fear of being fired by the bank's owner, her elusive boss, Karabraxos—who uses identical clones of herself, including Ms Delphox, to ensure the safety of her bank. Karabraxos is not averse to firing her minions when they let her down, which she does literally, by having them thrown into an incinerator.

Expensive tailored clothes

At first, the Doctor thinks a manipulative being known as the Architect has forced him into robbing the Bank of Karabraxos, along with Saibra and Psi. He eventually realizes, however, that he is the Architect himself, and that he's sent himself on a mission to infiltrate the bank in order to rescue the imprisoned Teller creatures.

## THE TELLER

Hard exoskeleton

Antennae project waves of invisible, paralyzing energy

Straitjacket prevents escape

Straps and buckles bind captive in a cage with jungle-like conditions

Cloven hoof

## SAIBRA

Saibra is afflicted with a mutant gene, which means she transforms into an exact replica of any life form that touches her bare skin. She, therefore, keeps herself covered up as much as possible, a situation that distresses her since it means she is always alone. Desperate to rid herself of her condition, Saibra agrees to help rob the Bank of Karabraxos in order to obtain a suppressant that will destroy her mutant gene once and for all.

Wrap keeps skin covered to avoid direct contact

All-black clothes suitable for robbing bank

Diodes and cables in head allow Psi to interface with other electronic systems

Data streaming visible in eyes during download

Fingertips project information

## PSI

An augmented human, Psi is a hacker-turned-bank-robber whose body has been upgraded with artificial parts. He once underwent a prison interrogation, and, worried that he might unwittingly endanger the lives of his friends and family, decided to wipe all memory of them from his mind. Now, like Saibra, he is after something precious that's stored deep within the vault of Karabraxos—a neophyte circuit that can retrieve lost data from any computer system, and will, therefore, restore his lost memories.

## Endangered Creature

One of only two surviving members of its species, the Teller is held captive in enforced hibernation by Ms. Delphox. When a security breach occurs, the Teller is woken up and forced to hunt down guilty intruders, using its telepathic powers to detect incriminating thoughts. The creature then paralyzes would-be robbers with a massive telekinetic charge, liquefying their brains and reducing them to brainless vegetables. In the end, thanks to the Doctor, the Teller is reunited with its mate, who has also been cruelly caged against its will.

# INDEX

Numbers in **bold** indicate main entries

**EDITOR** Emma Grange
**DESIGNERS** Rhys Thomas, Anne Sharples
**SENIOR DTP DESIGNER** Kavita Varma
**PRODUCER** Gary Batchelor
**MANAGING EDITOR** Simon Hugo
**MANAGING ART EDITOR** Guy Harvey
**CREATIVE MANAGER** Sarah Harland
**ART DIRECTOR** Lisa Lanzarini
**PUBLISHER** Julie Ferris
**PUBLISHING DIRECTOR** Simon Beecroft

**FROM THE BBC:**
Executive Producers: Steven Moffat and Brian Minchin
Drama Account Manager: Edward Russell
Brand Manager: Matt Nicholls
Script Editor: Scott Handcock
Picture Campaign Manager: Christine McLean-Thorne
Production Asset Manager: Stephen Nicholas

This edition published in 2015
First published in the United States
in 2014 by DK Publishing,
345 Hudson Street, New York, New York 10014

002–291223–Oct/15

Artworks: The TARDIS (pages 6–7) by Lee Binding; Sonic Screwdrivers (pages 22–23) by Peter McKinstry; Leadworth Map (pages 38–39) by James Southall; Dalek Flagship by John Maloney (pages 54–55); The Satan Pit by Richard Bonson (page 105); Pandorica Panel (page 146) by Peter McKinstry.

DK would like to thank Jason Loborik for his writing, Sam Bartlett and Pamela Shiels for design assistance, Julia March, Shari Last, Tori Kosara, and Cécile Landau for editorial help, Lisa Eyre for the index, and Neha Ahuja, Chitra Subramanyam, Umesh Singh Rawat, and Anant Sagar from the Delhi team.

www.bbc.co.uk/doctorwho
www.dk.com

A WORLD OF IDEAS:
SEE ALL THERE IS TO KNOW

STRAX

Collapsible multifunctional lorgnette device assesses medical wellbeing

Yellow lens diagnoses ailments

Red thermal sensor lens

Handle with on/off switch

Gadgets clip straight onto armored plating

Form-fitting battle armor